Single Parenthood

ISSUES
(formerly Issues for the Nineties)

Volume 8

Editor

Craig Donnellan

Independence
Educational Publishers
Cambridge

First published by Independence
PO Box 295
Cambridge CB1 3XP
England

British Library Cataloguing in Publication Data
Single Parenthood – (Issues Series)
I. Donnellan, Craig II. Series
306.8'56

ISBN 1 86168 152 6

Printed in Great Britain
The Burlington Press
Cambridge

Typeset by
Claire Boyd

Cover
The illustration on the front cover is by
Pumpkin House.

CONTENTS

Chapter One: Teenage Parents

Teenage pregnancy	1
Rate of teenage pregnancies is highest for nearly a decade	3
Teenage sexual health	4
Sex under sixteen?	6
One in four girls doesn't wait till 16 to have sex	7
Lost innocence	9
Teenage parenthood	10
Babies are for keeps	11
'I can't believe it's happened to me . . .'	13
Four births in 10 outside marriage	17
Don't stigmatise teenage mothers	18
Government launches £2m advertising campaign	19
The bitter regrets of teenagers who had under-age sex	20
The girls who do say no	21

Chapter Two: Lone Parent Families

Single minded	24
One-parent families today	26
The growth of lone parenthood	28
Rise of the single mother	31
Mamas and the papas	32
Today's challenge – to end lone-parent poverty	34
Brown reforms lone parent aid	38
Childcare alone not enough to get lone parents back to work	39
New nurseries to help single parents go to work	40
Additional resources	41
Index	42
Web site information	43
Acknowledgements	44

Introduction

Single Parenthood is the eighth volume in the **Issues** series. The aim of this series is to offer up-to-date information about important issues in our world.

Single Parenthood looks at teenage parents and one parent families.

The information comes from a wide variety of sources and includes:
Government reports and statistics
Newspaper reports and features
Magazine articles and surveys
Literature from lobby groups
and charitable organisations.

It is hoped that, as you read about the many aspects of the issues explored in this book, you will critically evaluate the information presented. It is important that you decide whether you are being presented with facts or opinions. Does the writer give a biased or an unbiased report? If an opinion is being expressed, do you agree with the writer?

Single Parenthood offers a useful starting-point for those who need convenient access to information about the many issues involved. However, it is only a starting-point. At the back of the book is a list of organisations which you may want to contact for further information.

*****

Teenage pregnancy

Information from the Social Exclusion Unit

Summary

Scale

In England, there are nearly 90,000 conceptions a year to teenagers; around 7,700 to girls under 16 and 2,200 to girls aged 14 or under. Roughly three-fifths of conceptions – 56,000 – result in live births. Although more than two-thirds of under 16s do not have sex and most teenage girls reach their twenties without getting pregnant, the UK has teenage birth rates which are twice as high as in Germany, three times as high as in France and six times as high as in the Netherlands. Some other countries – notably the US – have rates even higher than the UK. But within Western Europe, the UK now stands out as having the highest rate of teenage births.

Why it matters

The facts are stark:

- This is a problem which affects just about every part of the country. Even the most affluent areas in England have teenage birth rates which are high by European standards.
- But it is far worse in the poorest areas and among the most vulnerable young people, including those in care and those who have been excluded from school.
- Although less than a third are sexually active by the time they are 16, half of those who are use no contraception the first time, with hindsight most young women wish they had waited and for a significant group, sex is forced or unwanted.
- Teenagers who do not use contraception have a 90 per cent chance of conceiving in one year and those who do not use condoms are also exposed to a range of sexually transmitted infections (STIs). In a single act of unprotected sex with an infected partner, teenage women have a 1 per cent chance of acquiring HIV, a 30 per cent risk of getting genital herpes and a 50 per cent chance of contracting gonorrhoea.
- Of those who do get pregnant, half of under 16s and more than a third of 16 and 17-year-olds opt for abortion – that means just over 15,000 under 18s a year having an abortion.
- Ninety per cent of teenage mothers have their babies outside marriage, and relationships started in the teenage years have

> *Within Western Europe, the UK now stands out as having the highest rate of teenage births*

at least a 50 per cent chance of breaking down.

- Teenage parents are more likely than their peers to live in poverty and unemployment and be trapped in it through lack of education, child care and encouragement.
- The death rate for the babies of teenage mothers is 60 per cent higher than for babies of older mothers and they are more likely to have low birth weights, have childhood accidents and be admitted to hospital. In the longer term, their daughters have a higher chance of becoming teenage mothers themselves.

Why are rates in the UK so high?

In the 1970s, the UK had similar teenage birth rates to other European countries. But while they achieved dramatic falls in the 1980s and 1990s, the rates in the UK remained stuck.

However, there is no single explanation for their relative success and the UK's relative failure; individual decisions about sex and parenthood are never simple to understand.

But three factors stand out:

• The first is *low expectations*. Throughout the developed world, teenage pregnancy is more common amongst young people who have been disadvantaged in childhood and have poor expectations of education or the job market. One reason why the UK has such high teenage pregnancy rates is that there are more young people who see no prospect of a job and fear they will end up on benefit one way or the other. Put simply, they see no reason not to get pregnant.

• The second is *ignorance*. Young people lack accurate knowledge about contraception, STIs, what to expect in relationships and what it means to be a parent. Only around half of under 16s and two-thirds of 16-19s use contraception when they start to have sex, compared with around 80 per cent in the Netherlands, Denmark or the US. The reality of bringing up a child, often alone and usually on a low income, is not being brought home to teenagers and they are often quite unprepared for it. They do not know how easy it is to get pregnant and how hard it is to be a parent.

• The third is *mixed messages*. As one teenager put it to the Unit, it sometimes seems as if sex is compulsory but contraception is illegal. One part of the adult world bombards teenagers with sexually explicit messages and an implicit message that sexual activity is the norm. Another part, including many parents and most public institutions, is at best embarrassed and at worst silent, hoping that if sex isn't talked about, it won't happen. The net result is not less sex, but less protected sex.

These three factors point to a single faultline in past attempts to tackle this problem: neglect. Governments and society have neglected the issue because it can easily drift into moralising and is difficult for anyone to solve on their own. And the most vulnerable communities and young people have been the most neglected of all. Teenage pregnancy

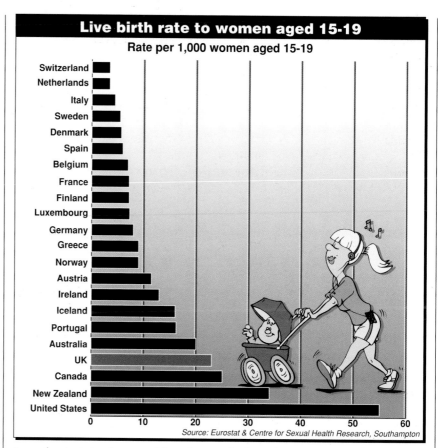

Live birth rate to women aged 15-19

Rate per 1,000 women aged 15-19

Source: Eurostat & Centre for Sexual Health Research, Southampton

is a classic joined-up problem but has never had an agency or individual prepared to take responsibility for tackling it as a whole.

Teenage parents: scale and trends

Scale

There are nearly 90,000 teenage conceptions a year in England resulting in 56,000 live births. Around 7,700 conceptions are to under 16s. This rate is higher than any other Western European country. The UK has not matched their success in reducing rates in the 1980s and 1990s. Ninety per cent of teenage births are outside marriage.

In 1997, in England:

• almost 90,000 teenagers became pregnant;

• roughly three-fifths went on to give birth, 56,000 in total;

• almost 7,700 conceptions were to under 16s (about 70 per cent to 15-year-olds), resulting in 3,700 births;

• 2,200 conceptions were to girls aged 14 or under; and

• around 50 per cent of conceptions to under 16s ended in abortion.[1]

A significant number of young women conceive more than once in their teens; one in six teenagers who had an abortion in 1997 had already had an abortion or a live birth, and 2 per cent had both.[2] One survey found that around one in eight young women who had their first baby in their teens went on to have a second child before they were 20.[3]

It is estimated that around 87,000 children in England today have a teenage mother.[4]

Four per cent of adult men and 13 per cent of adult women report having had a child under 20.[5] The difference is explained by the fact that partners of teenage mothers are typically between 3.5 and 5 years older than them.[6]

International comparisons

The UK has the highest rate of teenage births in Western Europe; twice that in Germany, three times that in France and six times the Dutch rate. The UK is nearer to the rates in other English-speaking countries, and the US and New Zealand rates are much higher.

The UK's ratio of teenage abortions is higher than in some comparable countries and lower than others.

The UK

Rates within the UK vary between the different countries. Scotland,

Northern Ireland and England have teenage birth rates of around 30 per 1,000 women. Wales is higher with a teenage birth rate of 37.7 per 1,000; this is similar to some areas in England.

Trends

Throughout most of Western Europe, teenage birth rates fell during the 1970s, 1980s and 1990s, but the UK rates have been stuck at the early 1980s level or above.

References

1 Office of National Statistics (ONS), *1997 Birth Statistics*, Series FM1, 1998.

2 ONS analysis of abortion statistic series, 1997.

3 K. Welling, J. Wadsworth, A. Johnson, J. Field et al *Teenage sexuality, fertility and life chances.* A report prepared for the Department of Health using data from the National Survey of Sexual Attitudes and Lifestyles, 1996.

4 ONS analysis of birth statistics series, 1997.

5 K. Wellings et al, op cit, 1996.

6 ONS analysis of birth statistics series, 1997.

Rate of teenage pregnancies is highest for nearly a decade

Advisory group demands sex education lessons for children aged eight

Teenage pregnancies have risen to their highest level in nearly a decade despite government initiatives intended to reduce the rate.

Figures released by the Office of National Statistics yesterday show that 101,500 teenagers became pregnant in 1998, compared with 96,000 the year before. Nearly half of teenagers who became pregnant were under 18; 8,438 were under 16. Today's teenagers are also increasingly likely to opt for an abortion, with 42 per cent choosing to do so in 1998, compared with 40.6 in 1997.

Teenage pregnancy campaigners said they were disappointed with the findings and urged ministers to be more realistic and pragmatic about what needs to be done.

Britain has the highest teenage pregnancy rates in Europe. The Government has pledged to halve teenage pregnancy rates by 2010 and is expecting to reduce the number of young girls who become pregnant this year by 2,000.

Alison Hadley, head of policy at Brook, a network of centres that gives advice on sex and contraception to young people, said: 'There is still a problem between the Government's health and education departments. They should be much more pragmatic and realistic . . . The sex and education guidance to schools should give teachers the confidence they need to educate children about sex at a young age.'

By Cherry Norton, Social Affairs Correspondent

She said sex education should start at primary school, as girls aged eight and nine were showing signs of puberty. 'Research has shown that young people are 50 times more likely to use contraception the first time they have sex if it has been discussed . . . beforehand.'

The figures showed that 47 in every 1,000 girls aged under 18 became pregnant in 1998 compared with 45.6 per 1,000 the year before, and only 44.6 per 1,000 in 1991. Abortion rates were highest in girls under 16 with more than half – 52.5 per cent – opting to terminate their pregnancy, compared with 49.7 per cent in 1997.

The rise in teenage pregnancies is not reflected among women in their twenties, where falling conception rates confirm the trend that most women are having children later in life. The number of women aged 40 and over becoming pregnant is now 35 per cent higher than in 1990.

The rise in teenage pregnancies during the Nineties has partly been blamed on the Pill scare in 1995, when fewer girls used the contraceptive after a warning that there was a higher risk of thrombosis.

A spokesman for the Department of Health said the rising rate of teenage pregnancy was not an indication of failed government policy.

'These figures were produced before the Government's drive has had time to become effective,' he said. 'We have appointed 150 coordinators, one for each health authority, to . . . develop strategies to reduce the teenage pregnancy rate. Education, publicity and the teenage co-ordinators will lead the Government's campaign to cut the rate.'

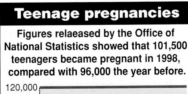

Teenage pregnancies

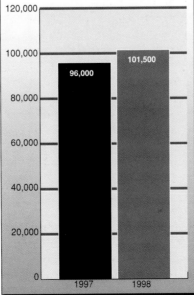

Figures releaased by the Office of National Statistics showed that 101,500 teenagers became pregnant in 1998, compared with 96,000 the year before.

96,000 (1997)

101,500 (1998)

Teenage sexual health

Information from Brook

What is the scale of the problem?

In England and Wales, during 1998, 101,000 teenagers became pregnant: a rate of 65/1000 15-19-year-olds, 47/1000 15-17-year-olds and 8.9/1000 13-15-year-olds. There were 425 pregnancies to under-14s.

In Scotland, during 1998, 8500 teenagers became pregnant, a rate of 67/1000 16-19-year-olds. There were 780 pregnancies to under-16s (8.6/1000 13-15-year-olds).

Fifty per cent of pregnancies to under-16s end in abortion. Ten per cent of teenagers have an abortion by the age of 20.

Teenage mothers and their babies face increased health risks. Although poverty is the strongest determinant of their health, being a teenage mother increases the risks for all social classes.

One in ten sexually active teenagers has a sexually transmitted infection.

The UK has the highest rate of teenage births in Western Europe: twice that in Germany, three times that in France and six times the Dutch rate.

Is the trend up or down?

Teenagers are less likely to become pregnant and almost half as likely to become a teenage mother today than they were 30 years ago. This is despite a steady increase in teenage sexual activity.

However, while other European countries have continued to reduce their rates, UK teenage pregnancy rates have not significantly declined since the early 1980s.

Although the average age of first sex is approximately the same in Western European countries, UK teenagers are far less likely to use contraception. Only 50% of under-16s in the UK use contraception at first sex, compared with 80% in Denmark.

How can we improve teenage sexual health in the UK?

International research has identified four factors necessary to reduce teenage pregnancy rates and improve sexual health:

- An acceptance of teenage sexuality and an openness of discussion;
- Effective sex and relationships education;
- Access to free, confidential sex advice and contraceptive services;
- A closing of the wealth divide.

The evidence

Openness

A comparison between England and Holland found that Dutch teenagers were far more likely than English teenagers to have a high level of confidence in talking to their partners about sex and contraception and to use contraception effectively at first sex. The contrast between Dutch and English boys was particularly striking. While English boys gave their reasons for first sex as 'peer pressure, opportunity and curiosity', Dutch boys cited love and friendship.[1]

A study of English teenagers found that those growing up in families where sex and relationships were discussed without embarrassment (the realist/humanist approach) had sex later than those from families where sex outside committed relationships was strongly condemned (the moralistic approach).[2]

Effective sex and relationships education (SRE)

Good, comprehensive SRE which starts before the onset of sexual activity does not make young people more likely to start sex. Instead it helps them to delay first sex and makes them more likely to use contraception when they start.[3, 4] Teenagers who are able to discuss

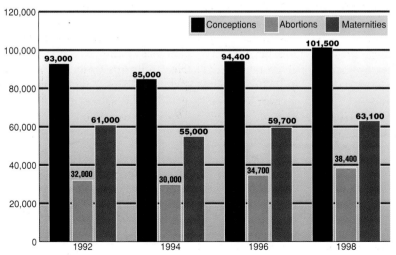

Teenage conceptions

Teenage conceptions in England and Wales 1992-1998 of girls aged 15-19. Conceptions leading to maternities or abortions.

Please note that the number of maternities and abortions for England and Wales are rounded up to the nearest 100 and as a result total conception figures for these areas may vary by up to 200.

Source: Brook

contraception with their partners before first sex are 5 times more likely to use an effective method.[5]

Ninety-six per cent of parents want schools to provide SRE. Moreover they want some aspects of SRE, such as discussion of contraception and visits to local services, to start at an earlier age than is currently outlined in the national curriculum.[6]

Access to free and confidential sex advice and contraceptive services

School SRE programmes are most effective in reducing teenage pregnancy rates if they are linked to local confidential contraceptive services.[3]

Teenagers who live less than 3km from a specialist young people's sex advice and contraceptive service are less likely to get pregnant than those living further away. They are also more likely to choose abortion if they do face an unplanned pregnancy.[7]

Young people have clearly identified the ingredients of a service they would trust:

- an accessible location, reached by public transport;
- opening times after school and at weekends;
- friendly, non-judgmental staff and explicit reassurance about confidentiality, particularly for under-16s.[8]

Contraceptive services without these features are likely to be viewed with caution and visited less.

Widening the availability of emergency (after sex) contraception is considered to be another way of increasing the effectiveness of contraceptive services in reducing teenage pregnancy rates. In one study where women were given a supply of emergency contraception to keep at home in case of a contraceptive accident, there was no increase in episodes of unsafe sex.[9]

Closing the wealth divide

The poorest areas in the UK have teenage pregnancy and birth rates up to six times higher than the most affluent areas. For example, in 1997, Walsall had a conception rate of 100/1000 15-19-year-olds compared with 31 in Kingston and Richmond. Among the under-18s, Lambeth has

the highest rate of 82/1000 and Rutland the lowest at 15/1000. Moreover, pregnant teenagers in more affluent areas are more likely to choose to have an abortion.

Although the vast majority of teenage pregnancies in these areas are unplanned, it is likely that a high level of unemployment and its effect on ambition is likely to undermine young people's motivation to use contraception effectively and delay having a baby.

What action is the Government planning?

After years of neglect of the problem of teenage sexual health, the Government has started to address the issue.

In England, *Teenage Pregnancy*, a report by the Social Exclusion Unit (1999), set a target to halve the under-18s conception rate by 2010. A detailed action plan is being implemented by a newly established, cross-departmental Teenage Pregnancy Unit.

A national sexual health strategy for all ages, currently being developed, will overarch the teenage pregnancy action plan.

In Scotland, the public health strategy outlined in *Scotland's Health, Scotland's Future*, recommends that Health Boards set local targets for a reduction in teenage pregnancy rates.

In Wales, *Better Health, Better Wales*, a strategic framework for promoting sexual health, currently

---

The poorest areas in the UK have teenage pregnancy and birth rates up to six times higher than the most affluent areas

---

out for consultation, aims to reduce the teenage pregnancy rates and the incidence of sexually transmitted infections.

In Northern Ireland, a sexual health strategy is currently under development.

Sources:

1. Ingham R (1998) *Exploring Interactional Competence: Comparative data from the UK and Netherlands on young people's sexual development.* Paper presented at 24th meeting of the International Academy of Sex Research, Sirmione, Italy 3-6 June.

2. *Development of an integrated model of sexual conduct amongst young people.* ESRC Senior Research Fellowship. End of Award Report. 1997.

3. Kirby D *No easy answers: Research findings on programmes to reduce teen pregnancy.* National programme for the reduction in teenage pregnancies, 1997.

4. NHS Centre for Reviews and Dissemination (CRD) Effective Healthcare Bulletin 3(1). *Prevention and reducing the adverse effects of unintended teenage pregnancies,* University of York, 1997.

5. Stone N & Ingham R (2000) *Young people's sex advice services: Delay, triggers and contraceptive use.* CHSR, University of Southampton.

6. Carrera C, Ingham R & Stone N (1998) *Exploration of the factors that affect the delivery of sex and sexuality education and support in and out of school.* CSHR, University of Southampton.

7. Clements S, Stone N, Diamond I & Ingham R (1998) Modelling the spatial distribution of teenage conception rates within Wessex. *British Journal of Family Planning* 24: 61-71.

8. *Someone With A Smile Would Be Your Best Bet: What young people want from sex advice services.* Brook, 1999, London.

9. Glasier A & Baird DT The effects of self-administering emergency contraception. *New England Journal of Medicine,* 1998, 339:1-4.
© Brook

Sex under sixteen?

New research questions official approach to teenage pregnancy. Children from broken homes twice as likely to be sexually active as those living with two parents

Britain has the highest teenage pregnancy rate in Western Europe, and official government policy is to reduce this. However, the findings of a major survey of teenage sexual attitudes and behaviour, published today by the Family Education Trust, calls into question the government's tactics. Official policy, under both Labour and Conservative administrations, has been to treat teenage pregnancy as if it is caused by ignorance of the facts of life coupled with the inability to obtain contraception. Both assumptions may be false.

The Family Education Trust's survey, *Sex Under Sixteen?*, is based on questionnaires completed by 2,250 students aged 13 to 15 between November 1999 and March 2000. They gave information on their lifestyles, their family backgrounds, their plans for the future, and their attitudes towards sexual relationships and family formation. The students came from 21 schools in different parts of England, chosen to give the sample a similar profile, in terms of social class, ethnicity, gender and educational ability, to that of the national child population.

Sex Under Sixteen? therefore represents an unusually large body of data on young people's attitudes towards sex, which is an essential component of any strategy to reduce teenage pregnancies.

Most under-age teens are not sexually active

One of its most important findings is that only a minority of under-16s – 17% in this large sample – are sexually active. Another important finding is that young people are still, on the whole, quite traditional in the way in which they view personal relationships, particularly in their own lives. 69% disagreed with the statement that 'marriage is old-fashioned and no longer relevant' and 89% saw their own lives in terms of getting married. 66% gave their reason for wanting to get married as the need 'to feel secure and loved'.

These findings have important implications for sex education. For many years this has been a controversial area of the school curriculum, with family organisations accusing sex educators of promoting 'alternative lifestyles' and ignoring marriage, while the government-sponsored sex education lobbyists argue that marriage is no longer relevant to many young people, and, when it comes to sex, 'they are all doing it anyway'. Clearly most students are not, and as they still have aspirations towards marriage, a better approach to sex education would help them to realise these.

The content of sex education programmes becomes particularly important in the light of claims from 45% of the students that school sex education represented the most important way they learned about sex – by far the largest group. However, while the majority felt that sex education gave them a better understanding of the physical and emotional aspects of sexual relation-ships, they were much more ambivalent on the question of whether it actually encourages sexual experimentation. 21% thought it did, while 33% disagreed. Those with sexual experience were twice as likely as those without experience to blame sex education for this.

'It just happened'

Amongst the most significant findings of the survey relate to the circumstances in which young people embark on sexual relationships. When asked why young people do not always use contraception when they have sex, the largest response (29%) was that 'sex is unplanned'. This is confirmed by the answers given by those who were already sexually active to the question: 'What was it made you decide to have sex that first time?' 30% (the largest group) said 'it just happened', 19% were drunk, 6% were talked into it by their partners, 3% cited peer pressure and a worrying 4% (all girls) said they had no choice. If we add these together, it seems that about two-thirds of these young people had not made a conscious decision to

engage in a sexual relationship. According to Robert Whelan, Director of the Family Education Trust:

'These answers put a great question mark over the official government policy on teenage pregnancy. Young people are not getting pregnant because they do not know where babies come from, or because there are not enough outlets to provide them with contraception. Of the girls in the sample who had been pregnant, 45% had either wanted to become pregnant or did not mind one way or the other. Only 12% of the sample thought that contraception was difficult to get hold of. Young girls are getting pregnant because they are drifting, or being pushed, into relationships which they are not ready to handle. This is the problem which has to be addressed.

'Only 17% of the young people in our sample were sexually active, but when we break down their responses, we find two very revealing

> *Young girls are getting pregnant because they are drifting, or being pushed, into relation- ships which they are not ready to handle*

factors. Firstly, the influence of the peer group was obvious. Only 4% of young people whose friends were not sexually active were sexually active themselves. Amongst those whose friends were sexually active, the figure was 43%. Secondly, the influence of the home was critical. Children from broken homes were twice as likely to be sexually active as children living with both parents.

'If the government is serious about addressing the problem of teenage pregnancy, it needs to address the underlying problem of the increasing number of children who are growing up in single-parent and other non-traditional family types. Funding groups which run teenage sex clinics will do little, if anything, to help, nor will more explicit sex education at younger ages. Indeed, the findings of our survey suggest that much government-sponsored sex education is already out of touch with young people's needs and aspirations, which tend towards marriage and stability. We must listen to what the young people in this survey are telling us, and help them to reach their goals in life.'

• *Sex Under Sixteen? Young People Comment on the Social and Educational Influences on their Behaviour* by Clifford Hill is published by the Family Education Trust, ISBN 0-906229-15-4, price £15.00, available from Family Education Trust, The Mezzanine, Elizabeth House, 39 York Road, London SE1 7NQ.

© Family Education Trust

One in four girls doesn't wait till 16 to have sex

> *By Jenny Hope, Medical Correspondent*

One girl in four has sex before the age of 16, the latest Government figures reveal. Back in the mid-Sixties, the number was closer to six in 100.

In other words, the proportion of girls having under-age sex virtually quadrupled between that decade and the birth of the Nineties, when the new statistics, which have only now been published, were collected.

But other figures also released yesterday suggest that over the past ten years, the rise may have become even more relentless than that.

In 1990, only one girl in every 50 under-16s visited a family planning clinic to seek advice or contracep-tion. By last year, that rate had also quadrupled.

The long-term impact of the revolution in morality which began in the Sixties, leading to a world in which sex between young teenagers

has become ever more commonplace, is made clear in two publications from the Office for National Statistics. Its figures also illustrate other key trends: how the proportion of births outside marriage has risen, as has the number of mothers who have never married, and how a 'Bridget Jones' generation have put off having a family until their late thirties, or never had one at all.

They also show how almost half the women in Britain who are under 50 are now unmarried, and how the ethnic minority population has risen.

The figures on teenage sex throw fresh light on medical evidence that diseases associated with promiscuity, such as chlamydia and gonorrhoea, are spreading among the young.

But by contrast, the statisticians show no corresponding leap in teenage pregnancies.

Their findings contradict the claims of the family planning lobby that young teenagers are woefully ignorant about such matters, suggesting that many are in fact fully aware of how to prevent an unwanted pregnancy. Since the mid-1970s, when GPs and clinics were first allowed to distribute free contraceptives, there has been only minor change in the figure for girls under 18 conceiving. The level is up by about an eighth, at around two in every 100.

Abortions performed on girls in the 14-17 age group have gone up by less than a third since that time, whereas abortion rates for women in their 20s have more than doubled.

Critics said yesterday that the enthusiasm of family planning organisations for spreading information about and access to contraception had done nothing to prevent sexual activity among girls who have barely left childhood, and who risk lifelong physical and psychological damage. Robert Whelan, director of Family and Youth Concern, said: 'There is far more conception than the figures show.

'But the extensive use of the morning-after pill is concealing the extent of the problem.

'There are all sorts of diseases such as chlamydia that cause long-term damage and which are a major cause of the present rise in infertility.'

He added: 'These teenagers are not really adults. They think they are, but in reality they are missing adolescence. They are being propelled into adult sexual relationships for which they are not ready, and which cause them long-term harm.

'This generation knows more about sex and contraception than any other generation in the history of the universe.

'The problem is a cultural one – that all the taboos that once used to protect people have gone.

'We won't solve it by giving more information to children – it is a matter of recognising that sex is not for children.'

Marriage

Almost four out of ten babies are born outside marriage – one per cent more than a year ago.

The rise in such births is directly linked to the number of lone mothers

In 1990, only one girl in every 50 under 16s visited a family planning clinic to seek advice or contraception. By last year, that rate had also quadrupled

who have never married, the statisticians indicate.

This suggests cohabitation often lasts only a few years.

The figures show that the number of single, rather than divorced, lone mothers began rising fast around 1986.

Overall, the proportion of women under 50 who are married has dropped to barely more than half.

Women now are twice as likely as their mothers to be single parents or to be childless.

The number of marriages is less than half that of 30 years ago, but there are some 1.5 million cohabiting couples in England and Wales.

Ethnicity

It was back in the mid-1950s that Government statisticians first began to try to count what was then known as the 'coloured' population.

In 1966, they put the 'New Commonwealth and Pakistan' population at a million. Estimates reached two million in 1980 following the migration of Asians from East Africa, which brought with it a

generation of dynamic families and individuals who achieved rapid economic success.

In 1991, the first national census to ask questions on ethnic origin counted just under three million people in the 'ethnic minority population'. Latest surveys show that minority numbers, recently swelled by the asylum seeker boom, are heading towards four million.

Bridget Jones

The birth rate overall has been plummeting and the number of childless women rising fast as more opt for careers and a single lifestyle.

One in five 40-year-old women is now childless, twice as high a figure as 20 years ago.

In a trend labelled the 'Bridget Jones factor' after the fictional diarist, who is in her mid-thirties with a chaotic career and love life, fewer women are having families in their twenties and more in their late thirties.

In the 1970s, seven out of ten babies were born to women in their twenties – now it is four out of ten. The number of women in their thirties having babies has nearly doubled. Over 25 years, the average age of a woman giving birth went up from 26 to 29.

Overall, 622,000 babies were born last year compared with 636,000 in 1998. Fewer have been born in recent times only in 1977 – when regular, predictable birth-rate cycles reached a low point – and during the war.   © *The Daily Mail, 2000*

The changing face of the family

There are approximately 16.3 million families in Britain. The total number of such families has grown over the last 40 or so years, although the number of households has increased at a much faster rate. This is mostly the result of more adults living on their own.

Percentages of people in households by family type, Great Britain		1961	1971	1981	1991	1998[1]
Couples						
	Dependent children	38	35	31	25	23
	Non-dependent children	10	8	8	8	7
	No children	26	27	26	28	28
Lone parents						
	Dependent children	2	3	5	6	7
	Non-dependent children only	4	4	4	4	3
Multi-family households[2]		3	1	1	1	1
One person households		11	18	22	27	28
Two or more unrelated adults		5	4	5	3	3
All families (millions)		13.7	14.5	14.8	15.7	16.3
All households (millions)		16.3	18.6	20.2	22.4	23.6

1 At Spring 1998. 2 Households containing one or more families.   *Source: Social Trends 29, 1999. Office for National Statistics (ONS)*

Lost innocence

**Teenagers who know too much too soon about the facts of life.
Second survey shows the scale of lost innocence.**

Teenagers are far more clued up about the facts of life than sex education lobbyists would have us believe, it emerged yesterday.

The great majority have a sophisticated knowledge that extends to the practical and legal details of obtaining and using contraceptives, an authoritative survey revealed.

Three-quarters of youngsters knew it was possible for those under the age of 16 to buy condoms.

The same proportion knew that a doctor was unable to inform a girl's parents if she asked for the Pill.

More than four out of ten girls had used the morning-after pill and seven out of ten knew how it should be taken.

Eighty-five per cent of the teenagers questioned said they intended to use a condom the next time they had sex.

The survey, sponsored by Channel 4 for a new series on sex among teenagers, was conducted by academics at Southampton University who questioned 1,000 youngsters between 14 and 19.

The results substantiated the findings of the Office for National Statistics which published a study earlier this week showing that sexual activity among teenagers had soared over the page 25 years, while the number of teenagers becoming pregnant had stayed roughly the same.

That suggested that most teenagers know how to use contraception, and are putting the knowledge into practice.

The Southampton research also largely reinforced the findings of the Government statisticians that one in four teenage girls had sex before the age of 16.

Its figure was 22 per cent. It also found that 15 per cent had had sex before their 15th birthday and one in 25 lost their virginity at the age of 13. More than a third were sexually experienced by the time they were 17.

By Steve Doughty, Social Affairs Correspondent

Among girls who had sex before the age of 16, 30 per cent regretted it. Half the teenagers said they were drunk when they lost their virginity and a third said the occasion was a one-night stand.

Two-thirds of the girls, compared with four out of ten boys, thought you should be in love before having sex – a figure that contrasts sadly with the 30 per cent whose first experience was a one-night stand.

Four out of ten teenagers who had not had sex said they had been under pressure to do so.

The research also suggested that teenagers were commonly engaged in behaviour that amounted to far more than sexual experimentation. A third reported having had sex a second time within a week of their first experience of intercourse.

The sex education lobbyists regularly claim that children and teenagers are alarmingly ignorant about sex and contraception and need much more advice and information.

But the ignorance factor was hardly apparent. Only one in ten teenage boys, as an example, believed that a girl could not get pregnant the first time she had sex.

Last year the Local Government Association, which represents social workers and council education chiefs, called for compulsory sex education in schools.

The great majority have a sophisticated knowledge that extends to the practical and legal details of obtaining and using contraceptives

It said 'ignorance' was one of the key factors in teenage girls becoming pregnant.

Earlier this month, the fpa organisation, formerly the Family Planning Association, launched a booklet to teach 14-year-olds the details of abortion, claiming 'young people are quite clearly telling us they want and need more information on all aspects of sexual health'.

But critics say too little is being taught about the dangers of early sex, including the potentially damaging psychological and emotional effects and the risk of hard-to-detect diseases like chlamydia.

The study found that ignorance of sex and contraception was concentrated in districts with high rates of social and economic deprivation.

Pregnant teenagers in these areas often went on to become single mothers, while teenagers from middle-class areas who became pregnant tended to have abortions.

Dr Roger Ingham, director of Southampton's Centre for Sexual Health Research, said: 'One reason for the good levels of knowledge of those in the survey was that it was conducted among teenagers still in full-time education. People who are out of education are much more likely to be less knowledgeable.'

Hugh McKinney of the National Family Campaign said: 'This research demonstrates that it is nonsense to say there are vast numbers of ignorant teenagers.

'The fact is that the vast majority of teenagers are very clued up about sex and contraception.'

But, he added: 'They get no guidance on what to do with this knowledge from their schools. That means that where they are ignorant is over the damaging effects of early sex in terms of disease, ill-health, and long-term psychological effects for young teenagers who are not ready to cope with adult pressure.'

© The Daily Mail, 2000

Teenage parenthood

Information from Barnardo's

'When I first realised I was pregnant I was in total shock. I didn't know how I was going to cope. That's why coming to Barnardo's was, well, such a lifesaver' . . .

Ruth aged 15

Statistics

- In 1997, 8,300 girls under 16 became pregnant[1].
- The UK has one of the highest rates of conception among girls under 16 in Europe – seven times the rate of the Netherlands[2].
- Fifty-two per cent of girls under 16 who become pregnant have a termination[3].
- Levels of knowledge among young teenagers about the facts of life and contraception are low[4].
- Men who learnt about sex at school are less likely to have sexual intercourse before the age of 16 than men whose main source of information has been friends or the media[5].
- Almost 1 in 14 young people have chlamydia, a sexually transmitted infection which frequently has no symptoms[6].

Background information

Low education levels, growing up in poverty and being a child of someone who was a teenage mother herself are all factors which increase the likelihood of girls becoming mothers in their teens. But it is not only poor, uneducated young people who become teenage parents.

One in seven girls currently leave care either pregnant or a mother, and half of young women become parents within two years of leaving care. Attention should be paid to the needs of children in the care of local authorities who are often very vulnerable in their relationships; may miss substantial parts of their education; and miss out on parental advice and support.

Young people who have been sexually abused or have been sexually exploited may also have difficulty in making positive relationships. Disabled children and adults are very vulnerable to sexual abuse. All children and young people, including young people with disabilities, have a right to skilled and sensitive education in the area of sexual health and relationships.

Barnardo's work

With young women

Barnardo's has 47 services working with teenage parents. Many have had the most destructive life experiences, little family support, and have little knowledge about health and protecting themselves.

We support young women who have recently left the care system and may be pregnant or already have a child. We help girls who become pregnant whilst still at school by providing support to enable them to finish their education and prepare for parenthood. These young women often have an erratic history of school attendance, yet most leave the unit having achieved a number of GCSEs and gained confidence and parenting skills.

Some projects work with very young parents, educating them about child care and helping them to develop parenting and practical domestic skills. In homelessness projects, many of the 17- to 19-year-olds attending for information and support are already parents.

Many of our projects include sex and health education in their work and some provide street work to reach young people who wouldn't otherwise have access to this type of information. We work with young people with learning disabilities on sexual health and have produced a training and video pack for parents and carers.

With young men

Young fathers currently receive little support or encouragement to stay involved with their children and few of the young women we see are in stable relationships with the father of their child.

There seems to be a general acceptance that a young woman becoming a lone parent is somehow inevitable. A positive concept of fatherhood and its responsibilities should be a key part of sexual and relationship education. Boys often feel left out of sex and health education because most of the focus seems to be on young women and avoiding pregnancy. Both boys and girls need to be encouraged to think about developing relationships and taking joint responsibility for sex and the consequences of having a child.

On average, it costs over £102,500 a year to run a project working with teenager parents.

Barnardo's views

- There should be a national strategy to deliver sex and health education to young people, with national standards to ensure consistency, accuracy and quality of information.
- Sexual health and relationship education should form a core part of the national curriculum.
- Structured training for teachers, social workers and youth workers should be provided which recognises that this is an area requiring distinct professional skills.
- Information and training for parents and carers should be available to help them to feel comfortable in talking to their

---

The UK has one of the highest rates of conception among girls under 16 in Europe – seven times the rate of the Netherlands

---

children about sex and relationships.

- Contraceptive and sexual health services should be designed to meet young people's needs.
- There needs to be better support for young parents and more encouragement for young fathers to be involved.

Further information

- Barnardo's produce leaflets and brochures covering all aspects of

our work today. Contact the information officer at Barnardo's, marketing and communications, Tanners Lane, Barkingside, Ilford, Essex IG6 1QG. Tel: 020 8498 7556, Fax: 020 8550 0429. Web site: www.barnardos.org.uk
- Family Planning Association (FPA), 2-12 Pentonville Road, London N1 9FP. Tel: 020 7837 54322.
- National Council for One Parent Families (NCOPF), 255 Kentish Town Road, London NW5 2LX.

Statistics:
1 Social Trends 1999
2 Office for National Statistics
3 BBC News Online 1998
4 'Supporting Families' – Home Office 1998
5 Family Planning Association 1997
6 Family Planning Association 1999

© Barnardo's
April, 2000

Babies are for keeps

Why does Britain have the largest number of teenage births in Western Europe? Jerome Monahan reports.

An alarmingly high level of pregnancies among young teenagers has led to the launch of a new government information campaign on the risks of under-age sex. Television soap operas are also tackling the subject by introducing controversial story lines about youngsters having illegal sex. But despite all this, many young people are still badly informed about the issue and Britain continues to top the Western Europe league table for teenage births.

What is the problem with Britain?

Children in the prosperous West seem to be experiencing puberty much earlier in their lives. They also experience sex for the first time at a younger age. But parental embarrassment and poor sex education has often left children in the dark about what is happening to them or how to handle relationships. Teenage births in Britain are twice as high as in

Germany and six times greater than the Netherlands where the age of consent is much lower than in the UK.

Is the problem getting worse?

No. The number of conceptions among the under-16s is fairly constant. It has fallen slightly since 1971 from 8.8 to 8.2 girls per thousand in 1997. Numbers of pregnancies among 12- and 13-year-olds are very small and also slowly falling. In 1997 there were 378 pregnancies among all girls under 14 in the UK.

Is pregnancy the only risk young people run?

No. Many young girls do not fall pregnant from unprotected sex but they and their partners are still taking big risks. The number of sexually transmitted infections among teenagers is rising. This is not surprising when between a third and a half of teenagers do not use contraception the first time they have sex and many carry on without it.

When should sex education begin?

The National Children's Bureau says children as young as three can be curious about sex. By the time most young people go to secondary school they are aware of a wide variety of issues including divorce, rape and prostitution. This suggests wide-ranging sex education cannot wait until key stage 3 when many children can be quite fixed in their behaviour and attitudes.

Should sex education just be about sex?

Critics such as the Sex Education Forum feel the topic is poorly taught in many schools since it is given too little importance in the timetable. In their view, effective sex education must tackle pupils' self-confidence, help them develop their relationship skills and deal with their confusions. This is also the Government's view and new guidelines about sex education were expected in schools before Easter 2000.

Does sex education encourage children to have sex?

No, research in 1995 by the National Health Service showed that young men are far less likely to have sex before 16 when the major source of their information on the subject came from specific school classes. Girls' behaviour did not alter either way after sex education classes.

Is teenage pregnancy only a matter of poor education then?

Poverty and lack of career opportu-

nities are an important factor. Childcare can seem very fulfilling when there are few other options. But most young women do not plan to get pregnant.

What happens to teenagers who get pregnant?

Under-age girls may well miss out on the antenatal (before birth) support that is available to women with planned pregnancies, according to the Brook sexual health charity. This can make birth an extremely scary and painful event. The new baby will then totally change the girl's life. In such cases, teenage fathers rarely help bring up their child – this is sometimes because of hostility towards them from the girl's family. Most girls will have to leave school once they have given birth. Some young mothers are lucky enough

to continue their education in special centres such as the Bristol Unit for School Girl Mothers, but there are few such places. A baby's birth signals the end of formal education for young mums and the start of a life of poor job prospects.

What changes are ahead?

The Government has promised to halve the number of under-18 conceptions before 2010. It is suggested their strategy has three messages: under-age sex is not a good thing; if you have sex use contraception; and if you have a baby when you are young you will get support to continue your education. Campaigns are being launched to help parents and teachers develop better communication about sex and education.

- Further details: the Brook charity is the UK's leading provider of services offering free, confidential sex advice and contraception to young people. Helpline: 0207 284 6040.

- First appeared in *The Guardian*, March 2000.

© *Jerome Monahan*

Dolls show realities of teenage pregnancy

By Nick Britten

Schoolchildren are being given electronic babies to demonstrate the reality of life with a baby in an attempt to curb Scotland's growing rate of teenage pregnancies.

Youngsters care for the 'baby' for one night and the doll is programmed to cry when it needs feeding, changing and comforting.

Susan Aglionby, commissioner of the Carlisle and the Scottish Borders Guides Association, which has signed up to the project, said: 'It is very easy for girls, particularly those from an unhappy family life, to think that a baby will give them something to love. The time and care that it requires is rarely brought home to them.'

However, Valerie Riches, of Family and Youth Concern, described it as a 'fad' in a misguided campaign that would do nothing to put young girls off having sex too early.

Ann Allen, convener of the Church of Scotland's social responsibility board, said: 'Until we really tackle lifestyle and self-worth issues teenage pregnancies are not going to stop.'

© *Telegraph Group Limited, London 2000*

'I can't believe it's happened to me . . . '

A ChildLine study on teenage pregnancy. By Gill Keep for ChildLine.

In 1997/98, ChildLine counselled 7,751 callers about pregnancy (434 boys and 7,317 girls). Approximately 55% of these callers were pregnant; others phoned because they were worried about being pregnant, or, in the case of boys, that their girlfriends were pregnant. Of those who gave their ages, 79% of young women were under 16. Their stories and concerns formed the basis of ChildLine's paper to the Social Exclusion Unit. A sample of 771 case records was chosen, which included young women from 12 to 18, young people in care, boys, girls who had been sexually abused and young parents. From these cases, some messages came through loud and clear about sex, relationships and pregnancy, and these enabled ChildLine to formulate recommendations to the SEU.

Who were the callers?
- ChildLine estimates that approximately one in four of all pregnant young women under 16 called for help and advice.
- Pregnancy was the fifth most common reason young women called ChildLine. However, for certain ages – 14- and 15-year-olds – it topped the list, and was only slightly behind family relationship problems for 16-year-olds. Children as young as 12 also phoned; some were in sexual relationships and worried about pregnancy.
- Of the 2,016 young people who told counsellors about their families (the rest gave no information), 60% lived with both birth parents, 25% lived with their mum and her partner, 6% just with their mother and 5% in a stepfamily.
- Sixty-one young women calling about pregnancy said they were in care.

ChildLine
0800 1111

- Counsellors talked to 434 young men. The records show a more complex picture than popular mythology of the feckless teenage father. Just as there were boys who wanted nothing more to do with the mother, so too were there boys who were concerned about their girlfriends, anxious to stand by them, and scared of telling their parents. They worried about supporting them financially, and about whether they were emotionally equipped to become a father at such an early age.

Recommendation 1
Set up a special helpline
- ChildLine's evidence suggests that one in four young women

under 15 who are pregnant call our service. They do so because it is uniquely placed to offer immediate, free and accessible help and support when they are at crisis point, or when they need to begin to come to terms with the fact of being pregnant.
- ChildLine is thus able to reach these particularly vulnerable younger women who do not seem to be contacting other agencies. A dedicated helpline offering information, advice and a non-judgemental listening ear would be of enormous help to young people.

Knowledge of contraception
- Whilst many callers mentioned contraception, they also told counsellors that they had had unprotected sex – highlighting a gap between theoretical knowledge and practice.
- There was little mention by young women of taking responsibility for contraception – where contraceptive methods were

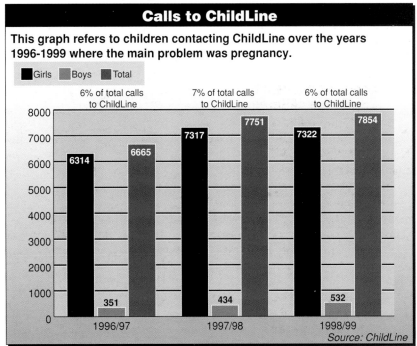

Calls to ChildLine

This graph refers to children contacting ChildLine over the years 1996-1999 where the main problem was pregnancy.

Girls | Boys | Total

6% of total calls to ChildLine | 7% of total calls to ChildLine | 6% of total calls to ChildLine

Year	Girls	Boys	Total
1996/97	6314	351	6665
1997/98	7317	434	7751
1998/99	7322	532	7854

Source: ChildLine

mentioned, in the majority of cases, they referred to condoms. This had the effect of leaving the girl vulnerable to the boyfriend taking responsibility.

- No one in the sample studied referred to their school as a source of information about sex education. Some mentioned the action that their school had taken as a result of them becoming pregnant, others talked of bullying and having to leave school. Others wanted to continue their school career. This does not mean, of course, that schools are not offering good sex education programmes, but it may mean that programmes are not being offered early enough, or in such a way that they affect the young people or make an impact.

Recommendation 2
Improve education about sex and relationships

- Sex and relationship education in schools needs to be more consistent and imaginative. Age-appropriate education should begin in primary school and continue as the child progresses through secondary school.
- School programmes should include, amongst other things, discussions on readiness to embark on sexual relationships, the emotional aspects of relationships, how to resist peer pressure, how and why to use contraception, and the implications and responsibility involved in being a parent.
- There should be an evaluation and expansion of peer-led school sex education programmes.

Getting help and support

- Of the 3,551 young women who told ChildLine whether they had told anyone about their pregnancy, 301 had told no one, 1,523 had told a friend, but only 336 had told their parents. Young people confided in each other abut sex and pregnancy. There was some evidence that young women turned to their partners for support, but on the whole, the evidence suggested that young people did not have or could not

find the emotional vocabulary to talk to each other about it.

- Telling an adult appeared impossible, and doctors were regarded with suspicion. Callers who mentioned visiting a doctor were very worried about confidentiality. They also reported that their doctor had suggested terminations when their pregnancy had been confirmed.
- Young pregnant women are as worried about the reaction of their parents as the fact of their pregnancy. A substantial number of callers talked of chaotic family lives, with physical and emotional abuse, siblings and parents misusing drugs and alcohol, and other teenage or young siblings with children. In these environments, callers had no confidence that they could confide in either parent and be listened to or supported.
- Even in households without additional problems, child callers described receiving aggressive and hostile responses and a lack of understanding from the callers' parents. However, it is interesting that the boys reported receiving a far less hostile response; in fact, some of the boys' parents welcomed his girlfriend into their home.
- Some girls as young as 13 and 14 are being thrown out of home when they tell their parents they are pregnant, with nowhere to go and no one to turn to.
- Young pregnant women who had multiple problems, like sexual abuse or homelessness, are particularly at risk to both themselves and their child. Seven young women who were pregnant and sexually abused were also actively involved in prostitution.

Young pregnant women are as worried about the reaction of their parents as the fact of their pregnancy

---

Recommendation 3
Develop accessibility of advice and information

- Young people must feel able to go to their doctors for advice and help in confidence. There is a need for training for doctors and nursing staff on confidentiality policy for young people under 16 seeking contraception. School nurses have a greater role to play in providing help and advice.
- Health service staff should be involved in bringing information about sex and contraception to young people, possibly through schools programmes, through the school nurse, or through special information sessions at health centres.

Recommendation 4
Offer help and advice to parents of young people

- Parents of young people need better information and advice on how to talk to their children, and help them manage their first relationships. The newly expanded ParentLine could be an important national source of advice for parents. Other initiatives should also be explored – for example, the use of schools in the evening to run special sessions for parents on sex and relationship education and how to talk to your children.

Some key themes from the study

1. Becoming pregnant

'I got drunk and had sex with a boy at a party.' (16)
'I had sex on Saturday with my boyfriend. He withdraw before coming but I'm still scared I'm pregnant.' (16)
'I got drunk for the first time and I had unprotected sex.' (14)

Young women of 16 and under are having sex in risky and unsafe conditions. Many callers told counsellors that they had unprotected sex, both those who described being in steady relationships, and those who had sex at a party, or at an unplanned event. Alcohol played a key role – getting drunk and then having unprotected sex. Peer pressure and pressure from their boyfriend also played a part in the caller's decision to have a sexual relationship.

Where contraception was discussed, only condoms were mentioned. This may be because some young women may feel happier about giving the responsibility of birth control to their boyfriend, who may well be older. It may also be the case that young people choose condoms for sexual health reasons, as well as for contraception. It may also be too difficult for a young woman under 16 to go to her doctor for the contraceptive pill, or any other form of contraception.

2. Reaction to being pregnant

The response of young women to being pregnant was very varied. Generally, young women were confused and frightened by their pregnancy, and full of apprehension abut the practical details, particularly how it might affect their relationship with their boyfriend and close family. Young women felt under intense pressure to decide what to do; they realised that they had a limited amount of time to think about the options and decide what was the best for them.

A few directly asked for information about terminations; others asked about adoptions and the implications of keeping the baby. About a dozen young women (13-, 14- and 15-year-olds) were quite definite that they wanted the baby, and their reasons ranged from wanting someone to love to feeling that they would be killing their baby if they had a termination. One young woman said, 'I'm too young for an abortion.' Others were torn, not knowing how to decide what to do, but describing how everyone else, their boyfriends, their parents, their boyfriend's parents, all had a view. A very small number asked about the morning-after pill – there appeared to be a very low level of knowledge about what it was and how to obtain it, or a hesitancy in asking the counsellor about it.

Most young women had told the boys about their pregnancy. Reactions differed: some boys immediately finished the relationship or refused to talk. In most cases, some communication was happening, but the level of confusion and distress shown by the caller suggested that the conversations were un-

helpful. Given the evidence and the fact that, in ChildLine's experience, boys find it hard to talk about their feelings and emotions (*We know it's tough to talk*, ChildLine 1996), it is likely that, when faced with such a crisis, the young people were unable to find the vocabulary to support and help each other through it.

3. Issues of confidentiality

'*I think I'm pregnant, but the doctor is my foster father's friend. I'm too embarrassed to see him – everyone will know and say I'm sluttish.*' (15)

There were only 128 direct references to doctors. This is likely to be an underestimate, as other callers may not have mentioned it. ChildLine is also unlikely to hear from callers who have received good advice and help from their doctors, so the sample may not be representative.

However, our evidence does suggest that young women under 16 are deterred from going to the doctor because of fears of confidentiality, and this may be impacting on the safety of their sexual relationships. Although the legal position allows doctors, with certain provisos, to provide confidential services to young people under 16, there was no indication that young women were aware of this, or that they trusted that the doctor would not break confidentiality.

4. Telling their parents

With a very small number of exceptions, young people were terrified to tell their parents. They feared their anger, their insults (being called 'slag' and 'slapper' is not uncommon), being beaten and even being thrown out of home. At a time when a young woman may be having to face the fact of being a mother, they feared, and some experienced, utter rejection by their own mothers. It is not surprising that parents were worried, angry and disappointed – fearing what pregnancy will mean for their own lives, as well as their child's. But it is disturbing to uncover the strength of their response and the impact that has on callers.

So scared are some callers that their fear leads to risky behaviour – 60 callers told counsellors they would run away rather than face their parents.

'*My dad threw my sister out when she got pregnant. He's hit her before. I'm so scared, I'm going to run away.*'

5. Vulnerable groups

Sexual abuse

Of 7,751 callers calling about pregnancy, 347 also called about sexual abuse. Of a sample of 94 studied in greater detail, eight were pregnant by their father or stepfather, three by their mother's boyfriend, one by her foster father and one by her uncle.

For these young women, pregnancy is just another problem to deal with, along with the general violence and abuse in their lives. They often phoned with multiple problems, and pregnancy was alluded to late in the conversation. Problems with alcohol and drugs also featured.

'Mum left last year. I'm being sexually abused by my stepdad. Now I'm pregnant. My stepdad got really angry when I told him and said I had to have an abortion.' (15)

Homelessness
Fifty-nine young people rang about pregnancy and being homeless. Time after time, young women between 13 and 18 told counsellors that they had been thrown out of home as soon as they became pregnant.

'I'm 15 tomorrow. I'm pregnant. The doctor told me I should have an abortion. My mum told me to get out and let Social Services put me in care. I just want to go home.'

'I'm five months' pregnant. My mum has thrown me out and taken my key away. I apologised to her, but she won't let me back in. The baby's father doesn't want to know.' (16)

Some callers said that they had been able to stay at friends' houses, but some were walking the streets and sleeping in the park. One 14-year-old had slept in a bus shelter the night before and was preparing to do so again that night.

Children in care
Sixty-one callers identified themselves as being in care and calling about pregnancy. The issues they raise are similar to other young women. However, there are worries and problems specific to their situations:
- They are worried that social services can insist on them having an abortion.
- They are scared that the foster family can make them have an abortion.
- They are scared the foster family will throw them out.
- They are worried about the reaction of their birth parents in addition to the foster family.
- They feel unable to talk to their foster parents, either because they don't get on, or because they do

get on and the caller does not want to jeopardise the relationship and risk losing an otherwise happy placement.

Children in care talk more of terminations and more of feeling trapped and unable to make a decision. There are far more adults in their lives who they feel would have a view and seek to influence them.

6. Reaching young men
'I want her to have an abortion, but she wants to keep it.'
'I'm 100% behind her.'
'She's not sure she wants to keep the baby, but I want to keep it – I've got the nursery all ready.'
'I love her, but I'm not old enough to have a baby. I can't afford to help, but I'll have to.'
'I've told her not to come near me again.'
'Will they put me in prison for having sex with someone under 16?'
'I'm scared to answer the phone in case it's her.'

Some young men called to say that they had been contacted weeks or months after having unprotected sex to be told that the girl was pregnant. They were in shock – 'gobsmacked' as one 15-year-old boy said. Some state that they never want to see their girlfriend again, while others are determined to stand by her and shoulder the responsibility.

The majority of male callers were in more long-term relationships where, again, often after unprotected sex, their girlfriend was now pregnant. Some were trying to persuade their girlfriend to terminate the pregnancy or to consider adoption – they did not feel ready to be fathers, were too young, taking their exams at school or not earning enough money to support a baby. But other conversations between the boy and the counsellor clearly showed the boy struggling to come to terms with becoming a father, and feeling both terrified and pleased.

Conclusion
Clearly, there is no one solution and any effective action must include professionals, schools, parents and young people themselves to have any chance of success. One of the major challenges is to promote a culture of openness in talking about sex and relationships and to encourage young people to seek help and advice without fear of judgement or condemnation.

• In late 1998 ChildLine was asked to submit a report on teenage pregnancy to the Social Exclusion Unit of the Government, based on calls and letters from young people. This report is based on that submission.

Four births in 10 outside marriage

By Steve Doughty, Social Affairs Correspondent

Four births out of every ten will be outside marriage by the end of 2000, new official figures revealed yesterday.

In the first three months of the year the figure reached 39.6 per cent – up by almost a full percentage point on the same period in 1999.

The 40 per cent barrier is certain to be breached later this year in England and Wales.

The new figures from the Office for National Statistics also bring bad news for the Government's campaign to cut the number of under-age mothers. They show that the number of girls becoming pregnant before their 16th birthday began to rise dramatically again last summer after a year in which under-age pregnancies had been falling.

The increase in the proportion of babies born to unmarried mothers reflects a trend going back at least 20 years.

It comes despite a welter of expert advice and statistics pointing to the difficulties faced by single parents and their children, who are now acknowledged as the poorest families in Britain.

Children of single parents are more likely than those of married parents to suffer illness, to achieve less at school and to face adult lives of crime, joblessness and single parenthood.

Although many children of unmarried mothers are born into cohabiting relationships, they still have generally worse life prospects. They also face a nine times greater chance than children of married couples that their parents will break up – throwing them into life with a single parent.

In the 1970s fewer than one baby in ten was born outside marriage and the figure 20 years ago was 12.8 per cent – one in eight. Since then the proportion has climbed more or less steadily to 21 per cent in 1986, 30 per cent in 1991, and 37 per cent in 1997, the year of Labour's election victory.

Family campaigners have criticised the Government for 'encouraging' the trend by abolishing the married couple's tax allowance and through Ministers' insistence that all kinds of families are equally good.

The disappointing figures on teenage pregnancies come despite a drive to encourage more teaching about sex and relationships in schools and youth clubs.

Taxpayers have been providing heavy finance to organisations like the Brook Clinics, which receives £4million a year from the state but sparked a row recently by publishing a 'good grope guide' to tell children as young as 14 the detailed mechanics of sex.

By early last year, the rate of under-age pregnancies was down to eight in every 1,000 girls under 16, from a peak of 9.1 in early 1998. But the new figures show a sharp rise in the second quarter of 1999 to 8.6 in every 1,000.

Just over half the pregnancies to girls under the age of consent for sex end in abortion.

The ONS findings, in the department's journal *Population Trends*, also showed that marriage rates are still declining. In the ten years to 1998, the number of married people fell by more than 1.3 million to 22.4 million.

Health dangers for teenage mothers

Teenage mothers are damaging their own health and that of their babies through ignorance of nutrition, experts said yesterday.

Many do not realise what their bodies need to cope with pregnancy.

And the fact that they often try to keep their pregnancies secret makes the problem worse, a British Nutrition Foundation conference heard yesterday.

More than 60,000 babies born to teenage girls each year have a higher risk of low birth weight and developing problems such as diabetes and heart disease later in life.

Professor Alan Jackson, of the Institute of Human Nutrition at the University of Southampton, told the London conference that babies born to teenagers weighed on average 200g less than those born to mothers of 20 to 24.

Dr Gail Goldberg, senior nutritionist at the BNF, said: 'We are really talking about old children rather than young women.

'Most pregnancies are unplanned so girls will not have been following advice to prepare their bodies. There is a fear that pregnant girls will restrict what they eat to avoid weight gain, either to keep themselves thin or to hide the fact that they are going to have a baby.'

A fifth of teenagers smoke, increasing the likelihood of damage to the unborn child. Fewer than one in six know the importance of taking folic acid before and during pregnancy – a deficiency in it is linked to an increased risk of spina bifida.

Teenage mothers are also more at risk of developing anaemia due to a lack of iron.

© The Daily Mail, 2000

> **In the 1970s fewer than one baby in ten was born outside marriage. Since then the proportion has climbed more or less steadily to 37 per cent in 1997**

Don't stigmatise teenage mothers

Information from the Policy Studies Insititute

A new report published today by the independent Policy Studies Institute, *Teenage Mothers: Decisions and Outcomes* by Isobel Allen and Shirley Bourke Dowling, provides a unique review of how teenage mothers think and behave during their pregnancies and after the birth of their babies. The research was funded by the Economic and Social Research Council (ESRC) and gives an in-depth account of how teenage mothers from three areas made decisions about becoming pregnant, continuing with their pregnancy and their housing and living arrangements. Professor Isobel Allen, co-author of the report, says:

'Teenage mothers should not be stigmatised and treated as a universal problem. They are not all lone mothers living on benefits in council housing. But our research shows that this does happen to a substantial number of them and there is certainly a need for better education in sex and personal relationships to help dispel romantic views of life as a teenage mother. Young men need to share the responsibility for teenage pregnancy and motherhood.'

'If I could live my life over again, I'd be working now and I wouldn't have a kid...'

'They make it sound like the council put you in palaces, but they don't... Who'd want to get pregnant for the sake of being put in a council flat?'

Among the key findings:
- The teenage mothers came from a wide variety of educational and social backgrounds and were not the deprived group of popular mythology.
- Few of them expected to end up as lone parents, in council housing or dependent on social security benefits. But a year after the birth:

- half of the women were no longer in a relationship with the fathers of their babies and one-fifth had no contact with the fathers at all;
- the overwhelming majority were on social security benefits with over half totally dependent on benefits; and
- one-third of them were in local authority housing with a further third on the waiting list.
- Most of them had not planned their pregnancies. They often reported being shocked or surprised to find they were pregnant even if they had not been using contraception.
- Few of them had considered termination of pregnancy. However, continuing with the pregnancy was often not so much a decision as an acceptance of what had happened, reflecting the sense of fatalism which characterised much of their subsequent behaviour.
- The babies' fathers often brought pressure on the women to continue with the pregnancy, even though the relationship foundered soon afterwards. Delight and joy at the thought of

becoming a father was often very short-lived.
- Nearly 50 per cent of the women said that their own mothers had been teenage mothers themselves. Only just over half of them said that their parents were still married to each other.
- The women's mothers were often helpful and supportive, but half of the women had not discussed the pregnancy with their mothers at all. Grandparents were often shocked and disappointed, but most gave total support to the women's decisions and did not try to influence them. However, many grandparents found themselves with increasing responsibilities after the babies were born.
- One of the main features of the research was the constantly changing pattern of relationships from the start of the pregnancy to the time the baby was a year old. Those who were still in a relationship with the baby's father were mainly married or cohabiting, while most of the rest were single and without a steady relationship.
- Two-thirds of the women had educational qualifications, mainly at GCSE level, but one-fifth had left school at 15 or younger. Nearly one-third were unemployed when they became pregnant compared with nearly three-quarters at the time of the interview. Two-thirds of them said they had changed their work, study or training plans as a result of the pregnancy.
- A quarter were receiving income support when they became pregnant compared with over 80 per cent after the birth.
- There was no evidence to suggest that women became pregnant to get council housing or social security benefits. Most of them

had known little or nothing about housing policy or benefits before becoming pregnant and the little they had known was usually wrong.

The report concludes that teenage motherhood often results in negative short-term outcomes in terms of relationship breakdown, financial hardship, dependence on benefits, lack of a social life, unexpected responsibilities, unsatisfactory housing, and difficulties in forming new relationships. But it must be remembered that this research found many young women who were happy with their babies, in stable relationships with young men who shared their responsibilities, were not on benefits and were living in their own accommodation. Teenage mothers should not be treated as a homogeneous group and

policy and services need to be flexible to meet their differing needs.

As a result, the report recommends:

- There is a need for better and more co-ordinated programmes of education in sex and personal relationships, geared to exploring feelings and emotions, as well as the roles and responsibilities of both men and women.
- Information should be made available about the likely short-term outcomes of teenage pregnancies and the reduced opportunities for teenage mothers to lead independent lives and have fun.
- Educational programmes should be related to the lives young people lead and want to lead. Romantic views of life as a

teenage mother should be dispelled by those who have had the experience of seeing their relationships hit the rocks and have been left 'holding the baby'.

- There should be a positive approach to reducing the adverse effects of teenage motherhood – not only to help lone parents return to work but to help all teenage mothers improve their education and vocational qualifications so that they can become more independent.

• *Teenage Mothers: Decisions and Outcomes* by Isobel Allen and Shirley Bourke Dowling is published by the Policy Studies Institute and is available from Grantham Book Services on 01476 541080. ISBN 0 85374 751 2.

© Policy Studies Insititute

Government launches £2m advertising campaign

By Andy McSmith, Chief Political Correspondent

The Government is launching an advertising campaign which tells teenagers the average age at which girls and boys lose their virginity.

While the answers may shock parents, ministers calculate that they might encourage schoolchildren to slow the headlong rush into sexual experience, as they discover that they are not as far behind the rest of the pack as they thought. The Government's new drive to persuade the young to be careful about sex coincides with a much larger and more expensive initiative to cut the number of single mothers drawing benefit.

Yvette Cooper, the minister for public health, has been advised that one of the main pressures on children is the often untruthful boasting of their classmates, which makes them imagine that they are the only ones in their year not having sex.

The £2 million advertising campaign, with its slogan 'Sex, Are You Thinking About It Enough?', will also offer teenagers advice on contraception and sexually trans-

mitted diseases. Ministers insist that they will not try to lecture children on keeping their virginity.

A Health Department spokesman said: 'The idea that it is cool to be a virgin was one option, but it was rejected. This has been thoroughly researched, and it has been found that lecturing children doesn't work. The point of the campaign is to give them facts not fibs. We know that teenagers think about sex an awful lot. This is to encourage them to think about it thoroughly.'

One of the main pressures on children is the often untruthful boasting of their classmates

The advertisements, which will appear principally in magazines aimed at the teenage market, are part of a larger £60 million campaign announced by Tony Blair more than a year ago, which has included the appointment of 100 'teenage pregnancy co-ordinators' who are running local initiatives to warn school teenagers about the pitfalls of unprotected sex.

At the same time, the Government is embarking on what Gordon Brown, the Chancellor, described yesterday as a 'new world of opportunity and choice for lone parents' by trebling the amount it spends on childcare in a drive to get single mothers off benefit and into work.

The number of lone parents drawing benefit has fallen by more than 100,000 in three years, but is still far higher, proportionately, than in most Western economies. The proportion of lone parents with paid jobs in Britain will soon be up to 50 per cent, but that compares with 82 per cent in France, 67 per cent in Germany and 60 per cent in America.

Margaret Hodge, the employment and equal opportunities minister, promised that there would be places available for 1.6 million children by 2004 – enough for every single mother living in an area of high unemployment. The Government would increase its investment in childcare from £66 million in the current year to £200 million by 2003-4, with 19,000 new child-minders getting grants to help them start up in business, and 900 new nurseries opened in deprived areas.

Mrs Hodge also said five experiments were to be launched in Cornwall, Ealing, Kirklees, Lancashire and York to test the ideas that childcare and nursery education should be provided on a single site. The announcement was welcomed by charities and pressure groups.

Kate Green, director of the National Council for One Parent Families, said: 'These are positive measures and an important step forward for the many lone parents who want to work.'

- The average age at which a girl loses her virginity is 17, and for a boy, 16, according to the Health Department.

The bitter regrets of teenagers who had under-age sex

The emotional and psychological damage caused by under-age sex is revealed in a study today.

It shows that nearly half of all girls under the age of 15 who have had intercourse regret the experience.

The largest UK survey of sexual behaviour in young teenagers shows that a fifth of young girls feel pressured into having sex by their boyfriends.

Less than a year after engaging in under-age sex, a high proportion of both boys and girls feel their sexual experience happened too early or should not have happened at all.

Nearly a third of girls feel they should have waited, and a further 13 per cent say that with hindsight they should not have indulged in sexual activity at all.

Among boys, 27 per cent believe they were not old enough to cope with having sex when they did, and five per cent think it should not have happened at all. Family values campaigners said the findings, published in the *British Medical Journal*, were further evidence of the need to protect youngsters from sex until they were old enough to cope with the emotional and physical consequences.

Other studies have shown that the number of youngsters under 16 who have sex is on the increase. Doctors have been alarmed at a sharp rise in the rates of sexually transmitted diseases in teenagers, some of which threaten fertility.

By Beezy Marsh, Medical Reporter

Experts estimate that as many as one in ten teenagers now carries a sexually transmitted disease. Up to 300,000 young people may be infected, with chlamydia and gonorrhoea the most common diseases.

Both are a major threat to fertility. As well as damaging the fallopian tubes, the diseases can also raise the risk of ectopic pregnancies and potentially life-threatening complications.

Promiscuous young women are risking infertility due to a 50 per cent rise in gonorrhoea over the past year, while chlamydia, which is often known as the 'silent disease' as it has no symptoms, is thought to affect one in 14 youngsters.

For the latest research, staff at the Medical Research Council Social and Public Health Sciences Unit in Glasgow studied more than 7,000 youngsters under 15, whose average age was 14 years and two months. A total of 18 per cent of boys and 15.4 per cent of girls in Scotland reported having sex.

The boys who most regret having under-age sex admit they exerted pressure on their girlfriend to go through with it.

Dr Daniel Wight, the senior research fellow who led the study, said: 'Studies have shown that when adults look back they often regret early sexual experiences, but until now it has never been clear whether this was simply an adult perspective.

'What is interesting is this is the first time that a group of children this age has been asked if they regretted it, and among the minority who had sex, many of them did.

'By and large, nearly half of the girls and a third of the boys are regretting having sex.' Dr Wight and his team plan to follow the group until the age of 20, to assess if there is any lasting damage from the early sexual experiences.

He said the findings were evidence that school sex education programmes need to equip children to be able to resist peer pressure.

'We need to give children the skills to avoid sexual experiences they don't want to have, or are likely to regret in the future,' he added.

Cornelia Oddie, of the campaign group Family and Youth Concern, said: 'This is yet more disturbing evidence of the negative effect of under-age sex on young people.

'The biggest concern is that society does not offer protection to these children.

'When we know about studies such as these, how can we still have Government-funded centres handing out contraceptives to children without their parents' knowledge?'

The girls who do say no

Teenage sex: the truth. Dolls which scream like real-life babies are the latest weapon against teenage pregnancies. Their effect is so powerful that many girls are vowing to protect their virginity longer.

This week, New Labour unveiled a multi-million-pound campaign to persuade young girls to treasure their virginity. The aim is to reverse Britain's position as having the worst record in Western Europe for teenage pregnancies.

The unmistakable cries of a baby fill the corridor of Broadgreen High School in Liverpool. Inside a nearby classroom, a gaggle of 14-year-old girls are desperately trying to soothe the screaming infant, but he will not be calmed.

They are still unsure of his name and decide, after some argument, to call him Lewis.

When the bell goes for break, they eagerly hand Lewis back to the teacher who, in turn, places him in a box along with five other babies. These are not real infants, of course, but aptly named 'ready-or-not tots', that have been sent to every secondary school in the city.

These electronic dolls, which simulate the behaviour of human babies down to the last burp, are part of an attempt to bring home the exhausting reality of rearing a child. Here, and across Britain's more deprived cities, they are becoming one of the main weapons in the battle against under-age sex and pregnancy.

Recent studies show that girls who live in impoverished areas are ten times more likely to get pregnant as a result of under-age sex. The logic is stark. If you have low aspirations and the future looks bleak, pregnancy is not a disaster. Alongside sex, it might even seem the best thing on offer.

Yet Liverpool, despite being among the poorest local health authorities in Britain, has kept the number of under-age teenage conceptions down to a relatively respectable level. It is on a par with far more affluent cities, that would not even consider using 'ready-or-not tots'.

By Rebecca Fowler

The latest figures show a rate of 8.8 conceptions per 1,000 girls. In other areas of Britain, where deprivation is widespread, including parts of South Yorkshire, Tyneside and South London, the rate is more than double this.

> *These electronic dolls, which simulate the behaviour of human babies down to the last burp, are part of an attempt to bring home the exhausting reality of rearing a child*

'There is no doubt that we are different,' says Dr Joyce Carter, a consultant to Liverpool local health authority. 'These figures are around the average, when you'd expect them to be among the highest in the country. It does seem that we might be doing something right here.'

So why exactly is Liverpool different? Are teenagers less sexually active than young people in other areas? Is the influence of the Church, in this traditionally Roman Catholic city, still a factor? Is the sex education that children receive superior? Are parents more closely involved? In short, are there lessons to be learnt here?

At this point, the experts take on whatever theory they champion, and enthusiastically suggest that is the key reason. Those who support making contraception as freely available as possible to the under-16s insist that improved junior family planning is the answer.

Those involved in the Church insist that the strong current of Catholicism, which still flows through Liverpool, means that parents and their children have much more respect for sex within marriage. That is still seen as an ideal among young Catholics.

In the meantime, the supporters of more comprehensive sex education from an early age, venture this is the key. Over the past seven years, Liverpool has led an intensive campaign. They have sought to reach every child in the city and educate them on relationships and sex. Their material and teaching methods were approved by the Roman Catholic Church.

The electronic babies at Broadgreen High School, are part of that programme. They already appear to be making an impact among the bewildered pupils of Year 10 (ages 14 to 15). Although it seems that their teacher is already preaching to the converted.

'I wouldn't want to take one of these home for the weekend, let alone a lifetime,' says one despairing 14-year-old girl, who is trying to fit the right key into the baby's computerised back to stop it crying. 'It would certainly put me off at this age. No thank you.

'But then I didn't need any putting off. There's more to life than getting pregnant when you're still at school isn't there?'

Aside from the hideous Sixties building which houses it, Broadgreen High is an impressive inner-city mixed comprehensive school. In the past seven years the headmaster has been praised for raising standards. Although it is in the middle of one of Liverpool's poorer estates, a significant number of pupils go on to university.

All the teenage girls that I spoke to were against under-age sex. Although most had boyfriends and girlfriends, and some had friends who had already experimented with sex, they claimed that they were apprehensive about rushing into it themselves.

So perhaps they are better qualified than anyone to honestly answer the question of what really deters under-16s from having sex. Aside from the risks of pregnancy and sexually transmitted diseases, the overwhelming message among the girls was that they simply did not feel ready.

One vivacious and articulate 14-year-old girl, Sarah Anderson, insists that it is about having the confidence

to say No to the traditionally more pushy boys. According to Sarah, who represented the school at a special meeting on sex education, teenager romances are fraught enough without the added pressure of sex. 'If you go out with a boy for more than a month, you're supposed to have sex,' says Sarah.

'Otherwise you get called boring. My last boyfriend went on and on about it. He'd point out these friends of ours, who we knew were having sex, and say: "Look at them, they're always doing it."

'I told him I just know I'm not ready yet. I'm not a pushover. No one can tell me to do something if I don't want to.'

One of the most confusing issues for teenagers is the mixed messages they receive about sex from sexually explicit magazines, films and music

---

Sarah met her boyfriend in the park in the summer, and he asked her if she would go out with him, if she was not seeing anyone else. She told him that she would think about it. Two days later he called her to ask her out a second time. She agreed and they went to see a film together.

They split up three months later after an incident when he told her he was going out with his grandparents for the evening when, she discovered the following day, he had gone to a local teenage club, Paradox, where he had tried to seduce one of her close friends.

This episode is written off with stylish nonchalance by Sarah. She was pleased, she said, that her friend told him to get lost.

But Sarah is clear about how the Government should be educating young people.

'The first thing is that when teenagers get drunk, they don't know what they're doing,' she says. 'I'm sure that's got as much to do with the

pregnancy rate as anything. That's when they're irresponsible. Teenagers get drunk a lot now, probably much more than they did in other generations.

'The other thing is talking about it more. Those dolls are a good idea, but only if you're talking about all the other stuff around it. There should be sex education lessons every year that you're at school, not just the odd video of a woman having a baby.'

One of the most confusing issues for teenagers is the mixed messages they receive about sex from sexually explicit magazines, films and music. On one side they are being told that sex is great, and on the other they are being told they are too young and it could ruin their lives.

'I saw this film called *American Pie* about teenagers,' says Sarah. 'And it said that if you were still a virgin when you left school, then there's something wrong with you. That's just more pressure.

'I know people who do have sex, but I don't. My mum and dad would go mad. In this magazine I read, a girl wrote in asking if your mum and dad can tell when you've had sex just by looking at you. I think they could. They'd see a difference in you and know.'

Sarah was mortified when her ex-boyfriend dialled her mother's mobile phone number by accident, instead of her own. He left a message, thinking it was hers, suggesting that they should 'take the relationship forward a step'.

Her mother was furious and Sarah was grounded for two weeks, before she was able to convince her parents that she had no intention of sleeping with her boyfriend.

'It's all about being confident enough to be your own person,' says Sarah. 'And I am.'

When Sarah leaves school she hopes to be an actress or a beautician. She also wants to have children one day, but not until she is around 25 years old. In the meantime, she is taking a break from boys.

'Of course, it's nice having all the attention when you go out with someone, and being able to say you've got a boyfriend. But that's different to being ready to have sex with someone. There has to be more to it than that.'

Teenagers in other European countries, where conception rates are dramatically lower than Britain's, are also convinced that there's more to sex than just the physical act. The most obvious example is Holland, where pregnancy rates are six times lower than in England and Wales.

At first it was mistakenly assumed that this was because the Dutch are so liberal. In fact, the opposite is true when it comes to under-age sex. When Dutch boys were asked to give their main reason for having sex, 56% said 'love and commitment', compared to 14% of boys in Britain. They appear to take it much more seriously.

And when adolescents in Holland do have sex for the first time, they are also much more likely to use contraception – 85% of teenagers protect themselves, compared to just 50% in Britain.

What Liverpool also appears to demonstrate, alongside other European countries, is that children who are brought up to discuss sexual issues and relationships openly, and from an early age, are much less likely to have under-age sex.

John Ashton, regional director for public health in the North West, says: 'What we know about Scandinavia, where sex education is very good, is that teenagers end up delaying having sex by about a year. When they have all the facts, and feel free to talk about it, they seem to opt for taking their time. There's no reason why that should not be the same here.'

The other key issue is giving teenagers the confidence to resist the potent force of peer pressure. For girls that usually means saying No to forceful boyfriends. And for boys, it means not feeling pressurised to show that they are one of the lads, by having sex.

The Family Planning Association (FPA) has been closely involved in the campaign to halve the number of teenage pregnancies by 2010.

According to chief executive Anne Weyman, the single biggest challenge is breaking through those pressures.

'The issue with teenagers is the difference between physical maturity and emotional maturity,' she says.

'There is a suggestion that girls are reaching puberty at a lower age, as young as eight years old, and that only serves to emphasise the difference.

'But the biggest single factor that makes you more likely to have sex in your early teens is social circumstances. If you can open doors for those young people who have low aspirations, you start to see their attitude to having sex change immediately.'

When the FPA recently worked with 14-year-old girls in Northern Ireland, the focus of the workshops was to give them a sense of ambition, beyond having a baby.

The results came at the end when the teenagers revealed that their attitudes had changed.

'When I went on the course at the beginning, I wanted to have a baby as soon as possible,' said one of the girls.

'But there are so many other things out there that I want to do and hadn't even thought of before. Now I don't want to have a baby until I'm 40!' The most encouraging sign is that children who are properly targeted on sex education appear to be receptive.

They respond with real enthusiasm, in Broadgreen High School in Liverpool, and already many have high hopes for their futures, despite the bleak surroundings of low-rise flats and crumbling terraced houses.

But the reality is still glaring. Even in Liverpool, the teenage pregnancy rates are woefully high compared to the rest of Europe and the US, where there has been a marked decline due to greater use of contraception, more comprehensive sex education and stringent welfare laws which don't offer teenage mothers easy access to social security payments.

Indeed, in Britain, the message is still not reaching enough teenagers.

As the girls in Year 10 hand back their 'ready-or-not tots', a handful reveal that they know local teenagers who have already had real babies.

'A girl in our road did and her boyfriend stuck by her and the baby,' says the 14-year-old girl. 'But I'd rather be able to pack it in its box for now.

You can't do that if it's real can you? I hope the boys are going to get a go looking after those dolls as well.'

Single minded

First J.K. Rowling, then Gordon Brown . . . We hear a lot about lone parents, but what is life really like for a solo mother on benefits? Diane Taylor investigates.

J.K. Rowling's £500,000 donation last week to the National Council for One Parent Families was more than just a goodwill gesture. The creator of Harry Potter, who is the mother of a seven-year-old named Jessica, has assumed the role of ambassador for this most put-upon of demographic groups. Speaking on behalf of the NCOPF, Rowling said it was high time that single parents were removed from the bottom of the social scrapheap. She was fed up, she said, with the hostile stereotype of single parents as 'feckless teenagers trying to get council flats'.

In reality, a mere 3% of Britain's 1.8m single parents are teenaged. Six out of 10 have been married and are now separated, divorced or widowed. But according to the council, 60% still live in poverty. The working families' tax credit has had some impact on single-parent employment, bringing the number on benefits down below 1m, but the government does recognise that the social exclusion many suffer remains a problem. This week, the Chancellor, Gordon Brown, announced plans in his next budget to help more single parents get off benefits and provide for their children through paid employment.

As a professional woman with a degree, Rowling had been shocked by the stigma she felt attached to bringing up her daughter alone. Despite teaching qualifications, and the support of friends from whom she could borrow money, she said it had been very difficult to haul herself out of poverty. Rowling acknowledged how much harder it must be for single parents who have none of her advantages. But what – behind the depersonalising statistics and

> **In reality, a mere 3% of Britain's 1.8m single parents are teenaged. Six out of 10 have been married and are now separated, divorced or widowed**

right-wing rhetoric – is life really like for a struggling single mother?

Debra Alexander, 38, knows all about the stigma attached to single parents on benefits. She lives in a three-bedroomed council house in north London with six of her seven children: Anthony, 18, Vanessa, 14, Michael, 11, Amelia, six, Terry, five and Robert, three. The eldest, Laura, now has her own flat.

'I remember when I was pregnant with Michael and one of the neighbours started tutting that I was on to my fourth baby and still not married. Another turned round and said: "Look at what some of the other kids in the neighbourhood do round here. They jump on cars and pull down trees. You never see Debra's kids doing anything like that. You only ever see them outside if she's with them. What's married got to do with it? It doesn't make anyone a better parent." I never heard any criticism from that neighbour after that.'

Alexander first became pregnant at 17 but having a child was hardly a passport to a comfortable

life of subsidised 'fecklessness'; instead, she and the baby's father were placed in a half-way house while they waited for a council home. 'We had to share a kitchen and bathroom with lots of others and just had the bedroom to ourselves,' she says. 'It was so disgusting that I kept running home to stay with my mum.'

When Laura was born, Alexander says that for the first few months it was like playing with a doll. 'I remember one day when Laura was eight months old. I had just bathed, dried and put powder on her when she peed and I had to start all over again. I got so angry with her and was seconds away from slapping her. I felt as if she had done it to me on purpose.

'Instead of hitting her, I cuddled her. And at that moment I realised that this tiny, innocent baby who hadn't asked to be born needed me for everything she was going to want in her life and that I was the one who was going to provide it. Everything changed after that and I became much more relaxed with my babies. None of them have ever been rushed through childhood.'

More children followed Laura and the family moved into their current home. 'I never got much help from the fathers of any of my children,' says Alexander. 'I think one of the reasons for that is that I learned to do everything myself. I remember climbing up to my loft, which doesn't have a staircase, a few weeks before Vanessa was born and lowering the pram down from there with one of the children's skipping ropes.'

Money has always been tight, but Alexander has become an expert financial manager and religiously saves child benefit for family treats and electrical goods. 'When Vanessa was a year and a half, I took the three children to Majorca. I had saved and saved to take them all and each time I collected the money I gave it to my sister Jill, who kept it in a bag in her freezer because she thought burglars would never find it there. It was such a lovely holiday and I cried my eyes out when we flew back into grey, rainy London.'

She has not managed a trip abroad with the children in the 12 years since. In other respects, through careful management of her resources, Alexander ensures that her children never go without. Still, she yearns to escape the benefits trap: her ambition is to be a midwife. Under various pilot schemes launched this week, lone parents will be able to study and train for up to 16 hours a week without losing benefits. But the big obstacle between Alexander and her dream is the £2,800 cost of a midwifery course.

'At the benefits office they are keen to get single parents back to work but they want you to take any old job to get you off their hands,' she says. 'I want to do something that I really want to do and that I know I'd be good at. I haven't had much encouragement there. But I will do it – with or without help. I'm saving up and one day I'll get that qualification and have my dream career.'

When Alexander was growing up she was never encouraged to aim high, and she is determined to instil different values in her own children. 'I saw Laura's old teacher recently and she asked what Laura was doing. She is doing really well now and studying for her accountancy exams, but she didn't do that well at school and was written off academically. The teacher had stereotyped her because of the family she came from and said to me, "I suppose she must have about three kids by now." She was very surprised when I told her she didn't and was working very hard.'

In spite of her circumstances, Alexander feels confident that she has always given her children the best in terms of love and guidance. 'I feel very proud to be my children's mother. Lots of people come up and tell me what a good job I've done

with them and I know they're right. I can tell from the way they love me and the way they play. They're not perfect but they're certainly 99%.'

. . . And the perks that go with a salary

Brenda Lewin, 49, has a 21-year-old daughter, Natalie, and a 10-year-old son, Jacob. She has managed to work while bringing them up.

'I split up from Natalie's father when she was four and had to find a job because I had debts and a mortgage. It took me a year to find something and then I landed a high-powered job in sales. I was earning lots of money: I could afford expensive holidays and that sort of thing. But I never saw Natalie and had to rely on a nanny to look after her.

'When I had Jacob I knew that I wanted to do things differently and took a part-time job managing a website so that I could work from home, collect him from school and be there to help with homework. I think flexible working is much more possible now than in the 80s. There's no question that things have worked much better this way round.

'Although we're not living in poverty on benefits, there are still plenty of drawbacks to being a single parent. The child of a single parent doesn't have a right of appeal against you which she or he would have if there were two parents around. That's something I'm really sorry about because I feel every child should have that right. Although friends have been very supportive, I feel terribly scared that we are on our own with no one to help us.

'And it's hard for children to live in two households. They wake up in the morning and think, which house will I be in later on and what do I need to take with me? There's a constant decision-making process, and I haven't got a husband to turn to to ask what he thinks we should do.

'On the other hand, it is wonderful to be able to make decisions without recourse to anyone. The freedom of being able to do that is fantastic.'

• First appeared in *The Guardian*, October 2000. ©*Diane Taylor*

One-parent families today

A summary report from the National Council for One Parent Families

A stage in the life-cycle

There are an estimated 1.7 million one-parent families in Britain today – about a quarter of all families.[1,2] They care for nearly 3 million children – just under one in four. Ninety per cent of lone parents are women.[2] One-parent families reflect changing family patterns throughout Western societies, with more couples cohabiting before both childbirth and marriage, and more divorce, re-marriage and stepfamilies. Although the divorce rate peaked in 1993, two in five marriages will still ultimately end in divorce.

The number of one-parent families has trebled in the last 30 years, with the most rapid increase from the mid-1980s – but this has recently slowed.[3] But in ten years there may be two million one-parent families.[4] A one-parent family is now a stage in the life-cycle, lasting about five years.[5] A third to a half of children will spend some time in a one-parent family.[6]

Society has been transformed since the creation of the National Council for One Parent Families in 1918, when the workhouse or the asylum were the only options for most unmarried mothers. But one thing remains the same: in the year 2000 just as in 1918, poverty is the main challenge for lone parents and their children. More than three in five lone parents in the UK live in poverty.

Routes into lone parenthood

In the nineteenth century a similar proportion of families was headed by a lone parent as today, but now most lone parents are divorced or separated rather than widowed.[9] Three in five lone parents are ex-married (divorced, separated or widowed). Lone fathers are mostly ex-married, usually divorced or separated; they are more than twice as likely as lone mothers to be widowed.

Another contributory factor is domestic violence. Thirty-five per

cent of lone parents have experienced violence in their last relationship with three-quarters of them sustaining physical injuries.[5]

Single mothers are separated cohabitees

The fastest-growing group of lone parents is now single or never-married lone parents; most of these, however, are ex-cohabitees and would be better described as separated. In 1998, nearly 38% of births were outside of marriage but four-fifths (79%) of these were registered by both parents. Three-quarters (77%) of these joint registrations were made by couples living at the same address.[11] Only 15% or one in seven lone mothers have never married or lived with their child's father.[3]

Divorce rates – on a plateau

According to *Social Trends*, the number of divorces involving couples with children under 16 peaked in 1993 at 95,000. Nearly three-quarters of decrees are granted to women, as more women than men petition for divorce. The most common reason for women to be granted divorce is unreasonable behaviour; for men it is adultery. In 1998, just over 150,000 children were affected by divorce, nearly twice as many as in 1971, but fewer than the highest figure of 176,000 in 1993. Around one in four were under five, and seven in ten were under 10. Almost one in four children born in 1979 ·had experienced divorce by the age of 16.

Gymslip mums

The average age for a lone parent is 34.[5] Lone fathers tend to be older, with the largest proportion in their forties; lone mothers are most likely to be in their thirties. At any one time, less than 3% of all lone parents are teenagers (about 40,000), although this is one route into lone parenthood.[13] Recent research has confirmed once again that there is

no evidence that teenage lone parents get pregnant to get housing and benefits. Most have little knowledge of housing or social security policy before getting pregnant and often what they do know turns out to be wrong.[14] Never-married lone parents tend to be younger than other lone parents and are more likely to be on benefit. However, they tend to have smaller families, take paid work and re-partner sooner.

Location

There are more one-parent families in inner-city areas and areas of industrial decline – for example, the North of England, Scotland and Wales, and some coastal towns. Nearly half (47%) live in Metro-politan county areas. These tend to be areas where there are poorer employment prospects and weaker growth in new jobs.

Ethnic diversity

On the latest figures, 11% of lone parents come from black or ethnic minority communities. However, some ethnic minority communities are more likely to experience lone parenthood, e.g. 55% of black families are headed by a lone parent, compared to 9% of Indian or 17% of Bangladeshi families and 22% of white families.[15]

In the year 2000 just as in 1918, poverty is the main challenge for lone parents and their children. More than three in five lone parents in the UK live in poverty

There is much research to show that ethnic minority groups experience much higher levels of unemployment and economic disadvantage.[16] However, black Caribbean lone parents are significantly more likely to be working and working full-time than any other group and less likely to be getting benefits. Bangladeshi and Pakistani lone parents tend to be older on average than other lone parents.

Responsibility for children

On average, one-parent families are smaller than two-parent families (1.7 children compared to 1.9),[2, 3] as a result of relationship breakdown when children are comparatively young. Single lone mothers have smaller families, with only 1.56 children on average. Forty per cent

of lone mothers have a child under the age of five.[2] This figure is higher for lone parents working under 16 hours a week and claiming Income Support (over 50%).[13] This reflects how difficult it is to work when you are a sole parent of young children. Lone fathers have older children; more than half are between the ages of ten and fifteen. By comparison, nearly 70% of lone mothers have children under 10, more than half of them under five.

Outcomes for children

Controversy surrounds the issue of how children are affected by relation-ship breakdown. Poorer socio-economic outcomes, educational achievement, health, behavioural problems and early parenthood have all been highlighted. However, in general, only a minority of children in separated families have poorer outcomes and there is no simple, direct relationship with family structure. An authoritative review of the evidence has drawn attention to the complex sequence of experiences before, during and after parental separation concluding that poorer outcomes are by no means inevitable.[17] Conflict, parental distress, loss of contact with a parent and repeated disruption all seem significant. Above all, the low income, poor housing and greater

Lone parents by sex and marital status, 1995-1997

Three in five lone parents are ex-married (divorced, separated or widowed). Lone fathers are mostly ex-married, usually divorced or separated; they are more than twice as likely as lone mothers to be widowed.

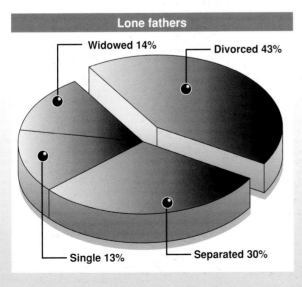

Lone fathers
- Widowed 14%
- Divorced 43%
- Single 13%
- Separated 30%

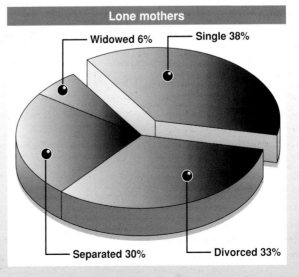

Lone mothers
- Widowed 6%
- Single 38%
- Separated 30%
- Divorced 33%

Source: ONS (1998) Social Trends 28, London: The Stationery Office

financial hardship experienced in one-parent families is, of course, crucial. A recent study found that in the absence of poverty, children from one-parent families fared no worse than children in other families.[18]

References
1 ONS (2000) *Social Trends 30*, London: Office for National Statistics, Crown copyright 2000.
2 ONS (2000) *Living in Britain: Results from the General House-hold Survey 1998*, London: Office for National Statistics, © Crown copyright 2000.
3 Haskey J (1998) 'One-parent families and their dependent children in Great Britain', *Population Trends 91*, Office for National Statistics, © Crown copyright 1998.
4 Family Policy Studies Centre (1999) *Family Policy – Autumn 1999*, Family Policy Studies Centre.
5 Marsh A, Ford R and Finlayson L (1997) *Lone Parents, Work and Benefits*, DSS/Policy Studies Institute, London: The Stationery Office.
6 Ford R and Millar J, Eds. (1998) *Private Lives and Public Responses: Lone Parenthood and Future Policy*, London: Policy Studies Institute.
7 Haskey J (1994 and 1999) 'Best estimates', *Population Trends 78 and 91 combined*, ONS, London: The Stationery Office.
8 Moss P, Holtermann S, Owen C and Brannen J (1999) 'Lone parents and the labour market revisited', *Labour Market Trends*, November 1999, ONS, London: Office for National Statistics, © Crown copyright 1999, and Holtermann S, Brannen J, Moss P and Owen C (1999) *Lone parents and the labour market: results from the 1997 Labour Force Survey and Review of Research*, Institute of Education, Sheffield: The Employment Service.
9 Snell K D M and Millar J (1987) *Lone Parent Families and the Welfare State: Past and Present, Continuity and change*, volume 2, part 3.
10 ONS (1998) *Social Trends 28*, London: The Stationery Office.
11 ONS (1999) *Population Trends 98*, Winter 1999, London: The Stationery Office.
12 ON (1999) *Marriage, Divorce and Adoption Statistics 1997*, London: The Stationery Office.
13 Hansard
14 Allen I and Bourke-Dowling S, (1998) *Teenage Mothers: Decisions and Outcomes*, Policy Studies Institute.
15 ONS (1999) *Social Trends 29*, London: The Stationery Office.
16 Platt L and Noble M (1999) *Race, place and poverty: ethnic groups and low income distributions*, York: Joseph Rowntree Foundation.
17 Rodgers B and Pryor J (1998) *Divorce and separation: the outcomes for children*, York: Joseph Rowntree Foundation.
18 Gregg P, Harkness S and Machin S (1999) *Child development and family income*, York: Joseph Rowntree Foundation.

The growth of lone parenthood

Diversity and dynamics. By Richard Berthoud, Stephen McKay and Karen Rowlingson

Since the 1960s, the number of families headed by a lone parent has grown significantly. This trend has been accompanied by other demographic changes such as increasing rates of cohabitation, births outside marriage and divorce. Although there has been much debate about the implications of the growth of lone parenthood, it has taken place in the absence of a fundamental understanding of the nature of that growth.

Research by Karen Rowlingson, Stephen McKay and Richard Berthoud has sought to fill that gap by investigating the increase in the number of lone parents in Britain over the last 30 years.

- Media reporting often exaggerates the prevalence of 'single' lone mothers. Only a third of all lone parents are never-married mothers and about half of these have separated from a cohabiting partner. The most common route to lone parenthood is still the separation of a married couple.
- The rise in lone parenthood is due predominantly to increasing numbers of women *becoming* lone parents, though there is also some sign of an increase in the length of time that women remain lone parents.
- Single women are more likely to become lone mothers if they come from poor socio-economic backgrounds. But for couples with children, it is their marital history and current situation which has the most influence on their chances of creating a lone parent family through separation or divorce.
- Single women rarely plan to become lone mothers and are not encouraged to do so by the prospect of social security benefits or council housing.
- Problems within couple relationships which lead to the formation of lone parent families often occur when the man becomes unemployed or the woman leaves employment to look after a newly-arrived child. In most cases, couples try hard to avoid separation: the commitment to marriage is not discarded lightly.

Introduction

The incidence of lone parenthood in the UK is now higher than at any time in the last two centuries, and is high in comparison with all other European countries. In the early 1970s, there were fewer than 600,000 lone parent families (Haskey 1994). There are now more than one and a half million lone parent families (Haskey 1998). The proportion of children living in a lone parent family rose from 6 per cent in 1972 to 20 per cent by 1994-5 (Central Statistical Office 1996).

The immediate causes of this growth include increasing rates of divorce and separation among couples with children, and more births to single women. The underlying causes are not so apparent, but include changes in social attitudes towards sex, contraception, marriage, and divorce; as well as changes in the relative economic prospects of young men and women.

The growth of lone parenthood has implications for aspects of social policy such as childcare, employment, housing and social security. It also raises concerns about the poverty and hardship experienced by lone parents and their children as well as the cost to the taxpayer of funding benefits for this group. There has been considerable discussion about these implications, yet we have no real understanding of the nature of the growth of lone parenthood. This research has sought to fill that gap by investigating the increase in the number of lone parents in Britain over the last thirty or so years.

About the study

The project focused on the entry routes into lone parenthood and its duration, in order to describe and explain the increase in the number of lone parents since the 1970s. Quantitative and qualitative methods were combined to make it possible both to measure the relative import-ance of various factors to the growth of lone parenthood and to explain the processes behind that growth.

The quantitative work involved event history analysis of life and work history data from the Social Change and Economic Life Initiative (SCELI). The data consists of around 6000 interviews carried out in six towns among respondents aged between 20 and 60 at the time of interview. Because complete life and work histories were collected, it was possible to analyse flows into and

out of different family types, including lone parenthood. The qualitative part of the project involved in-depth interviews with 44 women who were, or had recently been, lone parents. The interviews explored the stages that are involved in entering and leaving lone parenthood, and sought to discover how much choice people exercised over their changes in status.

Diversity and dynamics

The rise in lone parenthood is due more to increasing numbers of women becoming lone parents rather than to an increase in the time women spend as lone mothers.

Lone parenthood is a diverse family type and different factors influence the growth of single, as compared with separated, lone motherhood. Single women are more likely to become lone mothers if they come from poor socio-economic backgrounds. For mothers in couples, the main factors are the age at which they married, the speed with which they had children, and their partner's (rather than their parents') economic position.

The growth of lone parenthood has implications for aspects of social policy such as childcare, employment, housing and social security

---

Afro-Caribbean women are five times more likely than white women to have a baby while living on their own. Asian women are unlikely to have babies while single or separate from a partner.

Lone parenthood is a dynamic process which involves different stages. The study shows that some women experience only one spell of lone parenthood but others move in and out of lone parenthood through different routes. For example, they might originally become a lone parent by having a baby while single but then they might marry and later re-enter lone motherhood after separating from their partner. Lone parenthood is therefore a stage in family life rather than a permanent status.

The employment prospects of men and women

The single women interviewed for this study did not plan to get pregnant but, after becoming pregnant, some felt that a new life as a single mother would provide them with a role or an identity preferable to their pre-motherhood identity. Some of these women also felt that the fathers of their children would not make good husbands or partners (possibly because the men were unemployed or, at best, in irregular employment). The nuclear family *per se* was not being rejected, however, just the particular choices available at that time. Most of the single women interviewed said that they would have preferred to marry before having children, and the findings show that most single lone mothers marry quite quickly. Half marry within three years of having a baby.

The immediate causes of lone parenthood are different among separated lone parents. Those who had married young and/or had pre-marital conceptions were much more likely to become lone mothers than other women. And if the husband was unemployed, a couple with children was three times more likely to split up than if he was in paid work. All of the separated lone mothers interviewed had been in employment at some point in the past, and in some cases, difficulties of combining paid employment with domestic responsibilities, especially after the birth of a child, led to discord within the couple's relationship. Conflict over money was more likely to occur over control of money rather than over the level of income in the family. When a man became un-employed, money was short and so any conflict became more pronounced. Conflict also occurred when the woman gave up her job to look after a newly-arrived child; and in many cases the experience of non-employment was more problematic than having paid work.

The availability of social security and housing

It is widely believed that some women deliberately become lone mothers in order to receive social security and council housing. This study provides no firm evidence in support of that view. Single women got pregnant accidentally. Once pregnant, they knew that social security would be available to them in their own right if they became a lone parent and this enabled them to continue with the pregnancy. Decisions about whether or not to have an abortion were very complex, however, and financial issues were only part of the equation and usually only a minor part.

Separated lone mothers, on the other hand, placed greater hope on being able to find paid employment, although they also knew that social security would enable them to survive financially after separation. In situations where the man had left the woman, the existence of social security provided neither an incentive nor a disincentive for the woman to become a lone parent. It may, however, have enabled men to feel more at ease with the breakdown of their relationship, knowing that their families would be able to survive financially without their help.

None of the single women we interviewed appeared to have become pregnant intentionally in order to secure council accom-modation. During pregnancy, many remained living in the family home, where they enjoyed the support of their parents (especially their mothers). After their babies had been born, however, many single mothers eventually applied for, and were allocated, council accommodation. Separated lone mothers, on the other hand, generally stayed in their marital home and did not change their tenure or accommodation.

Sexual attitudes and behaviour

Most of the single lone parents we interviewed said that they did not plan to become pregnant, even though they either did not use contraception or used it ineffectively. This was generally because the risks of conception were believed to be low and outweighed by the risk of appearing promiscuous if they seemed well-prepared to use contraception. Single women left the responsibility to their male partners, who possibly assumed that the women were either on the pill or did not care about contraception. The study supported earlier views (Wellings et al 1994) that despite the relaxation in attitudes towards pre-marital sex, attitudes towards sex outside marriage have not changed. Extra-marital sex was generally condemned by separated lone parents, and while its discovery rarely caused an immediate separation, it was frequently a contributory factor.

The incidence of lone parenthood in the UK is now higher than at any time in the last two centuries

---

Relationship breakdown

In addition to infidelity, some couples separated because of domestic violence, while some men left their families seeking to recapture the youthful exploits they thought that early fatherhood caused them to miss. Most couples tried hard to avoid separation, however, often staying together several years after initial problems arose. But one of the more striking findings of the research concerned the degree of support given to lone parents by their own parents (especially their mothers). Some of the older generation had themselves experienced separation and lone parenthood, and could empathise with their daughters. Others had stayed in unhappy relationships and advised their daughters not to make the same mistake. Parents told their daughters to consider their own happiness above any duty they might feel to their partners and even, in some cases, to their children.

References
Central Statistical Office, 1996, *Social Trends*, 26, London: HMSO.
Haskey, J., 1994, 'Estimated Numbers of One-parent Families and their Prevalence in Great Britain in 1991', *Population Trends*, No.78, Winter pp. 5-19.
Haskey, J., 1998, 'One-parent families and their dependent children in Great Britain' in Ford, R and Millar, J *Private Lives and Public Responses: Lone Parenthood and Future Policy in the UK*, London: PSI.
Wellings, K., Field, J. and Wads-worth, J., 1994, *Sexual Behaviour in Britain: The national survey of sexual attitudes and lifestyles*, Penguin Books.

Further information

Richard Berthoud; Institute for Social and Economic Research, University of Essex. Stephen McKay; Policy Studies Institute. Karen Rowlingson; School of Social and Policy Sciences, University of Bath.

Rise of the single mother

By Steve Doughty, Home Affairs Correspondent

One in four families is now headed by a single parent, alarming new Government research revealed yesterday.

And nine in every 1000 families are headed by a mother who has never married and who has no steady partner, the figures reveal for the first time.

The proportion of one-parent families has leapt to 25 per cent from only 8 per cent in 1971, says the *General Household Survey*, which has been charting the British way of life for nearly three decades.

While the proportion of lone-father families has remained generally constant at less than three per cent of all families since 1971, the number of lone-mother families has more than tripled from seven per cent in 1971 to between 22 and 23 per cent.

In the mid-1990s there were signs that the increase in single-parent families was levelling off.

But publication yesterday of the full report for the 1998 survey shows that the proportion of single-parent families has in only two years risen to 25 per cent from 21 per cent in 1996.

The survey also counted for the first time the growing numbers of couples who choose to cohabit rather than marry.

Around one in nine people were cohabiting at the time of the survey in 1998.

As many as 29 per cent of unmarried women aged between 18 and 49 were living with a man. In 1979 just 11 per cent were cohabiting.

The proportion of women in that age group who were married dropped over the same period from 74 to 53 per cent.

The statistics point to a general pattern by which ever-rising numbers of children are destined to live without two parents, in family circumstances which mean they are more likely to suffer poverty and neglect, more likely to have a poor education, and more likely to fall into drugs, crime, unemployment and single parenthood themselves.

The figures led to renewed attacks on the Government's family policy yesterday from critics who say New Labour's dismissive attitude to marriage and the two-parent family has served only to push up the number of single parents.

The proportion of one-parent families has leapt to 25 per cent from only 8 per cent in 1971

Hugh McKinney, of the National Family Campaign, said: 'This is what happens when you pursue policies designed to discriminate in favour of single parents.

'Until the Government starts recognising marriage again through the tax and benefit systems, these figures will continue increasing, to the detriment of countless children and future generations.'

The number of single mothers has gone up by ten per cent since the mid-1990s, according to the new figures, and doubled since 1981.

The research also demolishes the widely-touted idea that few single mothers are young women without husbands or steady boyfriends and that many are widowed.

For the first time, the figures break down single parents into different categories, revealing that the continuing explosion of one-parent families is fuelled by growing numbers of young mothers who have never been married; by unparalleled divorce rates; and by the break-up of unmarried live-in couples.

Since the 1996 survey, the number of never-married single women has risen from seven to nine per cent of all families, while the proportion of divorced lone mothers has increased from six to eight per cent of all families with children.

The number of separated single mothers is steady at five per cent – one in 20 – of the overall total.

The survey's findings also backed up recent research that showed cohabitees nine times more likely to break up than married couples.

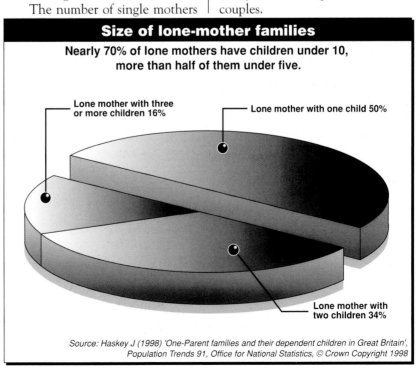

Size of lone-mother families

Nearly 70% of lone mothers have children under 10, more than half of them under five.

Lone mother with three or more children 16%

Lone mother with one child 50%

Lone mother with two children 34%

Source: Haskey J (1998) 'One-Parent families and their dependent children in Great Britain', Population Trends 91, Office for National Statistics, © Crown Copyright 1998

Among those who gave details of their relationships to researchers, nine in 100 had been through one previous cohabitation; three had been through two; and two through three or more cohabiting relationships.

The impact of family breakdown was also shown in the numbers of one-person households.

In the past, the great majority of people living alone have been elderly.

But in 1998, 29 per cent of all homes had just one person and nearly half of these – 13 per cent of the total – had one adult aged between 16 and 59.

The *General Household Survey* is regarded as the most authoritative study of life in Britain. Run by the Government's Office for National Statistics, it is put together from detailed questioning of 16,000 people living in 8,600 homes, which include 4,500 children.

The numbers of people involved are many times greater than those used by commercial opinion poll firms and the results correspondingly more reliable.

The findings on the fast increase in single-parent families come against a political background in which Government statements have engendered a view that all kinds of domestic arrangements are as good as each other.

Ministers have repeatedly insisted that it would be wrong to promote marriage because that would discriminate against 'other kinds of families'.

Jack Straw's National Family and Parenting Institute has disparaged marriage as irrelevant to most parents and the Home Secretary himself has given the assurance that 'whole generations' of children were brought up by single parents in the 20th century.

Analysis of the benefits system shows that single parents gain far more than married couples from state handouts, including Gordon Brown's Working Families' Tax Credit that helps single mothers into jobs but which does much less to encourage married families.

Tory social security spokesman David Willetts said: 'Most people do not choose to become single parents. We must do more to help them avoid becoming single parents if possible.

'We do know that if you are a single parent it is better to go out to work when your children are older.

'The Government is doing too little to encourage single parents with older children to take jobs.'

Mamas and the papas

Single parents get the best deal, says Barbara Ellen – you get a best friend, you get your child to yourself, and you get all the perks of being alone without feeling lonely

I hate the patronising way single parents are always portrayed as victims, when the truth is that it suits some of us down to the ground. Personally, I was born to be an SP. Not literally, of course – the midwife didn't say to my mother: 'Congratulations, it's a leech on society.' Nor did I plan it, it just seems to be my way. Thinking about it, everything in my life tends to err towards the solitary existence – I ran screaming from office culture into the shadowy world of home working, where I get to wear dressing gowns, one sock, and my fringe in a ponytail while pontificating grandly on life's mores. Similarly, I've never enjoyed men coming into my home, spreading their 'guy vibes', wiping their big bloke-boots all over my psychic space, until everything is gone and nothing is mine. So, these days, they don't. It's 'their place', neutral territory, or nothing. And 'nothing' and an ear-bashing about my alleged craziness is what I usually get.

Even with my friends, I'm like an agoraphobic space shuttle,

By Barbara Ellen

needing several weeks' notice to prepare for re-entry into the public orbit. It's not that I dislike going out, just that, nine times out of 10, bad things happen to me – or, should I say, bad things happen because of me. One of the side-effects of being a single parent is that you get childishly over-excited when other grown-ups are around, but I've got a hunch that for me it was always thus. To avoid arrest, and unexpected sex, I've learned to ration my congeniality, conduct 70 per cent of my social life on the phone, worship at the altar of 'alone'. It's like the ghost of Peter Cook is acting as social secretary in

> *That's the point, really. There's nothing remotely 'single' about being a single parent*

my head, readjusting his immortal line: 'I'm sorry you can't make that – you're watching television that evening.' The only difference is that now, 'alone' means me and my daughter. And that's a special kind of 'alone' – that's an 'alone' I'd be lonely without.

That's the point, really. There's nothing remotely 'single' about being a single parent. Just as with couple-parenting, you are never properly alone. Even when my daughter isn't home, she is with me in spirit, her essence hanging in the air like a bewitching perfume. Usually, this ghost-daughter is holding up a long list of 'Things Mummy Must Do To Keep Me Happy'. Or a series of Gillian Wearing-style placards, from the mournful ('I have nits – bad mother, you have failed me') to the opportunistic ('Buying a child's love has received a very bad press, but frankly I'd prefer it'), to the heartwarming ('After school, we will cuddle, watch *The Simpsons* and discuss the wonder of me, just like we always do'). When she is there physically, it is the same but different – a kind of colourful, knackering whirlwind of aimless mooching, crazed outbursts of activity (drama, choir, play-teas, sleepovers), and being sat on, 'because you're warmer than the chair'.

Isn't this what parents, single or otherwise, are for? Maybe not to be literal armchairs, but to be part of the furniture – cosy, unthreatening backdrops to the real deal of their child's life. When my daughter was born, I felt like I'd given birth to my best friend – but that's my reality, she may have other plans. Certainly, while she started off proclaiming that she wanted to marry me and live with me for ever, I have since been steadily demoted to the point where I am now living out my old age in a shed in her back garden, popping in occasionally as a kind of unpaid maid service. Soon enough, we will probably be talking in terms of nursing homes, or the gutter. I will be reduced to poignantly pressing my nose against the window of her life in the manner of Joan Crawford as the ditched mother in *Stella Dallas*. Alternatively, I could just stop being so melodramatic, and take up my rightful position on the sidelines, cheering my 'baby' on, jumping up and down with pride and excitement, screaming: 'Go, girl, go!'

That is one of the true perils of single parenthood. You're so used to being the main event, the dish *du jour*, of your children's life, it's odd to think that there will come a time when your screeched demands for them to finish their homework, clean their teeth and work towards becoming Leader Of The Free World may no longer be strictly necessary. The other perils of SP-dom are well documented – time and money are an issue for everyone, but, for single parents, it's as if Moses came knocking on your door, bearing a tablet of stone, reading: 'Nothing you do is good enough, you will never have peace of mind again.' When the government and society as a whole start joining in, waving their 'naughty stick' and tsk-tsking at the notion of familial breakdown, that's the point at which I, J.K. Rowling and every other single parent in the country blows a big, wet raspberry.

The logic behind the anti-SP argument is curious at best. If you're a couple with children, and you bring them up, then you're an icon of respectability. However, if you manage to do the same thing on your own, then you're an irresponsible idiot, and your children are sub-human spawn. As with everything, there's a wealth pecking order with single parents – some I know are far better off than me; others, like some of my best friends, are having it hard, through no real fault of their own.

As with everything, there's a wealth pecking order with single parents – some I know are far better off than me; others, like some of my best friends, are having it hard, through no real fault of their own

---

However, I'm sure all of us, male or female, rich or poor, media bore or teenager on council estate, would agree that being attacked ourselves is not so bad, but seeing our children vilified is hell on earth. Apart from the grinding poverty that afflicts so many of us, that's the main reason single parents get so depressed and angry. Call us all the names you want, wag fingers all you like, but don't sit around crucifying our children in your think-tanks and at your dinner parties. Do that, pal, and you're asking for a slap.

Of course, most of the time, single parents don't even think of things like that. It's just a hornet's nest buzzing away annoyingly in the mid-distance as, day by day, second by second, you deal with the real stuff of life. And all things considered – money problems shoved to one side, throbbing exhaustion shrugged off, childcare jigsaws falling apart – my life as a single mother in Britain Year 2K is pretty good. I get to be 'alone' without ever feeling lonely. I get to make all my decisions myself, without having to kowtow to some claustrophobic 'couply' committee. And, best of all, I get what all single parents get, by definition – the child. My daughter is beautiful, clever, funny and kind, a work of art all of her own making, and I get to hang out with her more than anybody else on earth. No one's ever going to convince me that I haven't got it made.

• First appeared in *The Guardian*, November 2000.

Today's challenge – to end lone-parent poverty

Information from the National Council for One Parent Families

O n separation or divorce, mothers and children usually see an average fall in their income of about £20 a week; by comparison, fathers are likely to see an increase of about £10 a week.[10] Like women in couples, lone parents find that caring for young children affects their ability to take paid work; some prefer to be full-time mothers or work part-time. The difference is that without a partner's income (and their help with childcare) many lone parents have to rely on benefits. With the exception of widows' benefits, help for one-parent families has always been through means-tested benefits paid at subsistence levels.

Typically, lone parents' incomes are less than half those of two-parent families, with average net incomes a little over £100 a week.[3] Fifty per cent of one-parent families live on gross weekly incomes of less than £150, compared to just 4% of married couples and 9% of cohabiting couples.[2]

The poverty figures

Lone parents have overtaken pensioners as the poorest group. Two-thirds of children in one-parent families are poor, compared with one-quarter of children with two resident parents. And a greater proportion of all poor children now live in one-parent families. Over 2.8 million individual lone parents and children live below the poverty line, up from 442,000 in 1979. Three in five lone parents (or 62%) live in relative poverty (defined as having incomes below half the average income after housing costs), up from 19% in 1979. By this measure, lone parents make up 20% of those in poverty, though they are only 8% of the population. This makes them the group at greatest risk of poverty in the UK. Now that there are more lone parents, this poverty is more visible; many would

argue that the social security system has strikingly failed to deal with family change.

The amount of money spent on children by parents has also become more unequal, rising only slightly in Income Support families and actually falling in non-working one-parent households. One explanation is that lone parents are likely to be out of work for longer periods due to family responsibilities. There is no starker evidence of the effect on children's living standards than this: the poorest fifth of the population has seen no real increase in spending on toys, children's clothes, shoes and fresh fruit for the past 30 years.[9]

Why are lone parents poor?

Being a mother with children costs money, and results in a loss of earning power. The Women's Unit estimates that a typical woman with GCSEs who stays at home for two years and works part-time for 12 will earn £241,000 less over her lifetime than a man with equivalent qualifications – the 'female forfeit'. She will also earn £140,000 less because she has two children – the 'mother gap'. For a woman with no qualifications the female forfeit is £197,000 and the mother gap grows to £285,000, if she takes nine years off work and works part-time for 28 years.[12]

The fact that most lone parents are women is key to understanding why so many one-parent families are poor. Women are likely to earn significantly less than men, to be in low-paid work, and are more likely to be employed in the non-standard or 'flexible' economy.[13] In addition, divorce and separation mean the further loss of any shared income.

Added to the costs of children is the lack of any independent

Family poverty

Lone parents have overtaken pensioners as the poorest group. Two-thirds of children in one-parent families are poor, compared with one-quarter of children with two resident parents.

Percentage and number of individuals below the poverty line by family type (i.e. the 'risk' and extent of poverty for each group).	% below poverty line	
	1979	1997/98
Pensioner couples	21%	24%
Single pensioners	12%	35%
Couples with children	8%	23%
Couples without children	5%	12%
One-parent families	**19%**	**62%**
Single without children	7%	22%
Total (all family types)	**9%**	**25%**

Source: DSS (1998) Households Below Average Income 1994-95-1997/98; and DSS (1999) Households Below Average Income 1994/95-1997/98, Leeds: Corporate Document Services

source of income other than earnings, with the exception of child benefit. This leads to reliance on means-tested benefits and their attendant unemployment and poverty traps. The lack of a second earner (or the potential for one) means that lone parents will almost always be worse off than couples.

Recently, lone parents experienced cuts in benefits partly compensated for (after an 18-month gap) by the introduction of the Working Families' Tax Credit (WFTC), including help with childcare costs and increases in Child Benefit. A review of housing finance and a national childcare strategy also promise to deliver more help, tackling two of the biggest barriers facing lone parents wanting to work – childcare and housing costs.

The Breadline Britain survey showed that 53% of children in one-parent families lacked three or more necessities compared to only 24% of children living with couples. Income Support provides only 70% of what is actually being spent on children in poor families and children in one-parent families are much more likely to be poor than children in two-parent families, whether or not their parent is working.[14] Lone mothers are 14 times more likely than other mothers to go without food themselves in order to meet the needs of their children.

Benefit cuts
The removal of the lone parent rate of Family Premium in April 1998 reduced Housing Benefit (HB) and Council Tax Benefit (CTB) for lone parents in paid work and for lone parents moving from Income Support into paid work. Government estimates for 1998/99 showed that up to 395,000 will have lost out. Working lone parents faced maximum average national losses of £10.20 per week. The losses in HB and CTB alone amounted to as much as £9.35 a week for some lone parents.[7]

Subsequent budget announcements introduced a number of welcome measures to help families with children; these went some way to restoring the losses. These changes

---

The fact that most lone parents are women is key to understanding why so many one-parent families are poor

---

were introduced over 18 months in November 1998 (a £2.50 increase in child personal allowances for under-11s), April 1999 (£2.50 increases in Family Premium and Child Benefit) and October 1999 (Working Families' Tax Credit and Childcare Tax Credit introduced and a further £4.70 increase for under-11s). Since October 1999 lone parents have also been able to keep all child maintenance when claiming WFTC, boosting in-work income. And, from April 2000, frozen lone parent benefit rates were slightly increased for the first time since the cuts.

The experience of poverty
On current benefit levels lone parents who have lived in poverty for some time cannot afford to eat healthily.[18] Many experience severe hardship, poor housing, health problems, lack of access to financial services, and debt.[19] Exposure to severe hardship has an adverse effect on employment. In one study, one-parent families in hardship in 1991 were found to be less likely to have jobs even four years later.[15] This suggests that the reduction in lone parent benefits will hinder return-to-work strategies.

Sources of income – benefits, earnings, child maintenance
Nearly three out of five lone parents (940,000) were getting Income Support in August 1999. Just over half of the remainder, about one in four (405,000), were claiming Family Credit (FC).[16] These are both means-tested benefits which are withdrawn as income increases, and so carry with them the risk of unemployment and poverty traps. More are likely to be entitled to Working Families' Tax Credit (WFTC) than claimed FC in due course.

When researchers set Income

Support against a meagre 'low-cost' budget, it falls short of meeting the needs of children in one-parent families by as much as £27 a week.[17] This situation is worse for younger lone parents who receive a lower rate of benefit under the age of 18. There is no help with mortgage costs for lone parents working more than 16 hours a week. Only one in three lone parents gets any child maintenance from their child's father.[3] Where child maintenance is due to be collected through the Child Support Agency (CSA), only 47% receive the full amount, 23% receive part-payment and the remaining 30% get nothing.[11]

Earnings
Recent Government policies have emphasised paid work as the route out of poverty for lone parents. Only 44% of lone mothers are in paid work, compared to 68% of women in couples with dependent children.[5] Having no paid work is closely associated with the incidence of poverty. According to the London School of Economics, only one-fifth of the increase in child poverty in one-parent families can be attributed to the rise in the number of children living with lone parents – the increase is more closely linked to the lone parents having no paid work, up from 30% in 1968 to 58% in 1995/6.[9] But the inadequacy of benefits is also significant.

Nine out of ten lone parents are women and, according to the New Earnings Survey, three-quarters of the low paid are women and two-thirds of low paid workers are part-timers. Over half of low paid workers are women part-time workers. For many working lone parents having a job is no guarantee of being free of poverty. Working lone parents on FC get an average hourly rate of pay of £3.60 though FC brings the hourly reward for work up to £7 an hour.[3]

The contribution made by earnings to lone-parent incomes is quite small, with wages representing only 36% of gross household incomes on average, while benefits make up 52%.[1] For the eight out of ten lone parents in receipt of means-tested benefits, these make up three-quarters of their income.

The barriers to paid work include:[4]
- the attitudes of employers and the organisation of work;
- lack of transport;
- existing financial hardship and the constraints it imposes;
- lack of access to childcare, both formal and informal;
- lack of skills, confidence and work experience;
- low pay and scarce and insecure jobs;
- concern about meeting housing costs;
- the complexity of the benefit system.

Why don't they get a job?

Although 90% of lone parents say they would like to work at some point, this does not mean that they are 'work-ready' straight away. It is estimated that about three in ten are already working nearly full-time, three in ten are ready to work, three in ten will work one day and one in ten will never be able to work.[4] For many lone parents this is not through choice but because of the difficulties of combining work with caring for children alone.

Many find they have to leave work on becoming a lone parent because it is too difficult to continue.[20, 5] Three in ten non-working lone parents state that their own ill health or disability makes it difficult for them to work. A quarter of lone parents say that a child has a long-term illness or disability of some kind.[3]

Lone mothers also differ in their views on parenting: some are committed to being the primary child-carer, at least for a time, while others, such as black lone mothers, often see paid work as the best way to provide for their families.[23]

Lone mothers with children under five are the least likely to be in paid work, with half as many working either full- or part-time. With older children, rates of full-time working catch up considerably, but compared to women in couples part-time seems to be a much more difficult, albeit the preferred, option.

Lone parents in the UK have high childcare costs compared to other countries because of the low level of public subsidies. Research into lone parents' employment in 20 countries identified high childcare costs as the main reason for our low rates of lone-parent employment.[24] Only one child in every 7.5 under the age of 8 has a registered childcare place.[21] Seventy-seven per cent of lone parents say that lack of childcare prevents them leaving Income Support and almost two-thirds say that paying for childcare is a problem.[22]

Housing

On becoming a lone parent, 58% move, most commonly into local authority accommodation.[20, 8] Many stay with family friends or relatives before finding a new place to live; 30% of one-parent families have been homeless within the past 10 years compared to only 3% of couples with dependent children.[6] Two-thirds of lone parents live in rented accommodation, usually social housing, compared to less than a fifth of other families.[2] Only a third are owner-occupiers compared to three-quarters of couples.

The challenge to policy-makers

The statistics are not the whole picture and individual lone parents

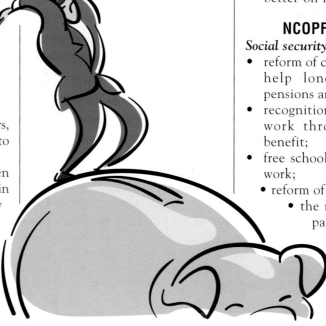

will continue to make different decisions about paid work, childcare and so on. The diversity of lone parents' lives is often as striking as the similarities. Sadly, lone parents have often been portrayed simply as a burden on the social security budget, and their 'welfare dependency' referred to as if it were a personal choice. In fact, policies have practically institutionalised poverty for lone parents, and they are paying the price for the scant progress this century in righting this injustice. The Government has committed itself to eliminating child poverty within 20 years – we await the results with keen interest.

Lone parenthood is usually a temporary stage; policies should address the problems caused by the lack of an independent or second income and the difficulties of combining paid work with unpaid caring responsibilities during this period. The other key problems are the unemployment and poverty traps resulting from means-tested benefits, and the unequal and low pay of women. Solutions include:
- meeting more of the direct costs of children;
- acknowledging the indirect costs of children by valuing unpaid caring work;
- developing a guaranteed maintenance system; and
- tackling low and unequal pay and helping lone parents to be better-off in paid work.

NCOPF advocates:

Social security
- reform of contribution rules to help lone parents access pensions and benefits;
- recognition of unpaid caring work through a parenting benefit;
- free school meals for those in work;
- reform of the Social Fund;
- the reversal of the lone parent benefit cuts;
- tackling the low-paid poverty trap;
- help with extra costs when moving into work.

Maintenance

- a system of child maintenance payments guaranteed to lone parents;
- more maintenance to be ignored when calculating benefits;
- exemption for lone parents when they or their children are at risk, and abolition of the benefit penalty;
- improvements to CSA administration, particularly in collection and enforcement.

Childcare

- more help with the costs of children and childcare;
- childcare of the highest quality to meet the requirements of lone parents;
- help with costs extended to those working unsociable hours or in education and training;
- more help with childcare for those with larger families and disabled children.

Help in paid work

- measures to make it easier to take paid work and be better off working;
- measures to tackle the low and unequal pay of women;
- improved maternity provision and paid parental leave;
- family-friendly employment.

Education and training

- a greater emphasis on education and training in the New Deal for Lone Parents and 'ONE';
- improved access to and help with the costs of education and training.

Housing

- reform of help with housing costs to include mortgages, reduce the poverty trap and to compensate for lone parent benefit cuts;
- action to change housing allocation policies which force lone parents and children to live in some of the worst accommodation.

References

1. ONS (2000) *Social Trends 30*, London: Office for National Statistics, Crown copyright 2000.
2. ONS (2000) *Living in Britain:*

Results from the General Household Survey 1998, London: Office for National Statistics, © Crown copyright 2000
3. Marsh A, Ford R and Finlayson L (1997) *Lone Parents, Work and Benefits*, DSS/Policy Studies Institute, London: The Stationery Office
4. Ford R and Millar J, Eds. (1998) *Private Lives and Public Responses: Lone Parenthood and Future Policy*, London: Policy Studies Institute
5. Moss P, Holtermann S, Owen C and Brannen J (1999) 'Lone parents and the labour market revisited', *Labour Market Trends*, November 1999, ONS, London: Office for National Statistics, © Crown copyright 1999, and Holtermann S, Brannen J, Moss P and Owen C (1999) *Lone parents and the labour market: results from the 1997 Labour Force Survey and Review of Research*, Institute of Education, Sheffield: The Employment Service
6. ONS (1998) *Social Trends 28*, London: The Stationery Office
7. Hansard
8. ONS (1999) *Social Trends 29*, London: The Stationery Office
9. Gregg P, Harkness S and Machin S (1999) *Child development and family income*, York: Joseph Rowntree Foundation
10. Jarvis S and Jenkins S P (1998) 'Marital Dissolution and Income Change: Evidence for Britain', in: Ford R and Millar J, *Private Lives and Public Responsibilities*, London: Policy Studies Institute
21. CSA (1999) *Quarterly Statistics*, November 1999, London: The Stationery Office
12. Rake K (ed.), Davies H, Joshi H, Rake K and Alami R (2000) *Women's incomes over the lifetime,*

Women's Unit/Cabinet Office, London: The Stationery Office
13. McKnight A, Elias P and Wilson R (1998) *Low Pay and the National Insurance System*, Manchester: EOC
14. Middleton S, Ashworth K and Braithwaite I, *Small Fortunes: Spending on children, childhood poverty and parental sacrifice* (1997) York: Joseph Rowntree Foundation
15. Bryson A, Ford R and White M (1997) *Making Work Pay: Lone mothers, employment and well-being*, York Publishing Services
16. Own estimates derived from *Income Support Statistics Quarterly Enquiry*, August 1999, DSS; and *Family Credit Statistics Quarterly Enquiry*, August 1999, DSS
17. Parker H (1998) *Low Cost but Acceptable: A Minimum Income Standard for the UK*, Family Budget Unit, Bristol: The Policy Press
18. Dowler and Calvert (1995) *Nutrition and diet in Lone Parent families in London*, Family Policy Studies Centre/Joseph Rowntree Foundation
19. Kempson E (1996) *Life on a Low Income*, York: Joseph Rowntree Foundation
20. Bradshaw J and Millar J (1991) *Lone parent families in the UK*, DSS, London: The Stationery Office
21. Daycare Trust (1999) *A Childcare Guarantee: a new deal for parents, children and employers*, Briefing Paper 4, London: Daycare Trust/TUC
22. Shaw A, et al. (1996) *Moving off Income Support: Barriers and Bridges*, DSS, London: The Stationery Office
23. Duncan S and Edwards R (1999) *Lone mothers and paid work: gendered moral rationalities*, London: Macmillan
24. Bradshaw J, et al. (1996) *The employment of lone parents: a comparison of policy in 20 countries*, Family Policy Studies Centre/Joseph Rowntree Foundation

---

Lone parenthood is usually a temporary stage; policies should address the problems caused by the lack of an independent or second income

---

- The above information is from the National Council for One Parent Families. See page 41 for their address details.

Brown reforms lone parent aid

Government offers extra money, childcare places and employment flexibility to get people back to work

By Larry Elliott and Charlotte Denny

The chancellor of the exchequer, Gordon Brown, will today launch a partnership between Whitehall and business to provide jobs for lone parents as the government declares its intent to make help for the family central to next year's Budget and a key dividing line in the forthcoming election.

Scorning Conservative plans to scrap Labour's tax breaks for the working poor in favour of a married couple's allowance, Mr Brown will unveil plans for extra money, additional childcare places and more flexible jobs to raise the proportion of lone parents in work to American levels.

'We want to see a sea change in the opportunities available to lone parents,' he will say in Bristol at the launch of the Treasury's pre-budget report consultation period, which will lead to extra assistance for poorer families in next spring's Budget. 'We want to give lone parents real choices, enabling them to move from welfare to work and out of poverty.'

Five of Britain's leading firms – Morgan Stanley Dean Witter, Schroder Salomon Smith Barney, Sainsbury, Direct Line and Granada – have agreed to be the trailblazers for the scheme designed to tempt lone parents back into the labour market with family-friendly working practices.

Government figures show that the number of lone parents on benefit fell from 1,015,000 to 910,000 in the three years from May 1997 to May 2000, raising the proportion in work from 43% to 50%. However, Mr Brown is concerned that this is still a much lower figure than in the US, where it is heading for 70%, and France, where it is 82%. The chancellor believes that getting lone parents back to work is the best way of tackling child poverty, where Britain's record is still one of the worst in the developed world.

As part of this drive, Mr Brown will today provide details of pilot schemes which allow lone parents to choose between education or training, working for less than 16 hours a week without losing all their benefits, or working longer hours and taking advantage of the working families' tax credit, the earnings top-up for low-income households. Mr Brown will confirm that the working families' tax credit is to be made more generous and announce an advertising drive to encourage low-income workers to apply for it.

The government's labour market policies for the working poor will be praised today by the Organisation for Economic Co-operation and Development. The OECD says the working families' tax credit and the new deal, programmes which the Conservatives have pledged to scrap, have been instrumental in attracting lone parents back into the market.

'Tens of thousands of lone parents in Britain find work worthwhile for the first time because of the working families' tax credit,' the OECD's director for employment, John Martin, will tell a conference in London on social exclusion.

The Conservative party's pledge to replace the tax credit with the old family credit benefit will cost 1m families nearly £25 a week, according to the chancellor. 'Scrapping the working families' tax credit and the new deal for lone parents would deny lone parents the choice of going out to work and would leave millions of children and their parents in poverty,' Mr Brown will say today.

Mr Brown's aides made it clear yesterday that new measures for lone parents were high on the agenda for next month's pre-budget statement.

With the opposition making the traditional two-parent family the centre-piece of its approach, the government is determined to show that its welfare reforms have delivered benefits to both one-parent and two-parent families.

As part of the government's campaign, the employment minister Margaret Hodge will today announce 1m extra childcare places will be available by 2004 as a result of a threefold increase in funds to over £200m.

Childcare alone not enough to get lone parents back to work

Information from the Policy Studies Institute (PSI)

Most out-of-work lone parents say they are not able to take paid jobs even if they could find affordable childcare. Other pressures keep them at home, according to new research from the independent Policy Studies Institute.

The report, *Childcare in the Balance* by Reuben Ford, examines whether lone parents really are locked out of the labour market by the lack of affordable childcare. The study found that while just half the out-of-work lone parents said that the cost or lack of childcare was stopping them going back to work, other things were more important:

- Only five per cent said the cost of childcare was the only serious barrier they faced and just two per cent said the availability of childcare was the sole obstacle to employment.
- Six in every seven out-of-work lone parents who cited problems with childcare reported another problem that needed to be solved first, before it would be possible for them to work.
- The biggest reason given for not seeking work was because their children were too young and needed their mother at home (42%). Nearly one in five (18%) said this was their only reason for not working.
- Many recently separated lone mothers were still adjusting to their new situation and felt that going out to work could be more of a threat than an advantage.
- Out-of-work lone parents had a lack of confidence in their own skills and in their ability to compete in the labour market. This problem increased the longer they had been out of work.
- Lone parents felt that few suitable jobs were available to them and some reported that employers discriminated against them.

The study was based on a national survey of 850 lone parents and in-depth follow-up interviews with 57 lone mothers. It compared the relative importance of the many barriers to work facing lone parents. Among the third of lone parents who had become so only recently, several needed time to get used to their new circumstances. Marie, a divorced mother of three, said 'I think that's the worst of it. It does take a long time to get used to being on your own and being able to cope with children on your own.'

> **'Every time a lone mother thinks about returning to work, she has to consider whether the job will earn enough to compensate for the costs of childcare'**

Women who were strongly motivated towards work remained so throughout their marriage, parenthood and lone parenthood. Others who had preferred to remain at home with their children before becoming a lone parent, found it harder to see themselves in a new role, bringing home a wage but spending less time with their children. They doubted whether the advantages of work outweighed the quality of the childcare they could themselves give to their children. Lone parents were also deterred from work by their own lack of confidence, and what they saw as discrimination against them by employers. Sally, a separated mother of two, said:

'I hadn't got the confidence. I hadn't worked for seven years and these were all new skills. I was going into a totally new environment. I'd never been in an office before. I didn't know what they were like.'

Others said they had been turned down by employers wary of taking on staff without partners to share caring responsibilities. Dr Ford concludes that lone parents are faced with a difficult balancing act between the demands of the labour market and the supply of affordable childcare: they have to assess the skills demanded by a prospective employer, how much they will be paid and the needs of their children who are already coping with the strain of separation.

'Every time a lone mother thinks about returning to work, she has to consider whether the job will earn enough to compensate for the costs of childcare and whether it will still enable her to spend quality time with her children to compensate for the hours she will have to spend away from home', he said. 'We must accept that some lone mothers will choose not to work despite the severe hardship they may experience or the incentives to work we can provide.'

The research was funded by the Department of Social Security. Other key findings:

1. Two-thirds of working lone parents use childcare. Of those who use childcare, 42 per cent pay for it, on average one-fifth of their after-tax earnings.
2. Of those out-of-work lone parents who say they would need childcare if they were to enter work, two-thirds expect to pay for it.
3. Most lone parents had heard of Family Credit, but fewer (55%) had heard of the childcare allowance. Those who did know about it found it difficult to understand.

© Policy Studies Institute (PSI)

New nurseries to help single parents go to work

By Marie Woolf, Chief Political Correspondent

A new childcare initiative, including a million extra nursery places, was announced yesterday by ministers in the biggest investment in helping single parents to return to work.

More than 900 new nurseries are to be set up in deprived areas of England in a £155m injection of funds into childcare over the next four years. Annual investment in childminding and after-school clubs will also rise, from £66m this year to more than £200m by 2003-4.

Margaret Hodge, the Education and Employment minister, said that almost 40,000 people would be offered start-up grants to set up as childminders in the next two years.

The rise in funds for childcare comes on top of a financial package revealed by Gordon Brown to help single parents to get back into work.

The Chancellor announced a £4.35 a week rise in working family tax credit for parents with two children and a new child tax credit worth £1.5bn for 5 million qualifying households. Another new programme, called Choices, will offer £15 a week on top of benefit for people going into training or education.

The Government believes that giving access to childcare is the solution to helping parents to return to work, and that tripling the budget for nursery care will address the nationwide shortage in qualified childminders.

Ms Hodge said: 'We are witnessing a revolution in childcare for families up and down the country. Never before has a government attempted to deliver so many new childcare places.

'For decades mothers have been telling governments of all colours that what they want is good quality childcare. This is not about forcing anybody into work. It's about giving mothers who want to work real choice.'

The Chancellor said the Government believes that the new package of support for single parents could find jobs for 70 per cent of them. A pilot scheme starting this month, which will be extended throughout England next year, will allow parents to take part-time jobs of less than 16 hours a week and keep the first £20 of wages without affecting income support.

> ### 'These are positive measures, and an important step forward for the many lone parents who want to work'

'We want to give lone parents real choices, enable them to move from welfare to work and get them and their children off benefits and out of poverty,' Mr Brown said.

Labour has created almost 300,000 childcare places since coming to power in 1997. The extra money will provide places for 1.6 million children.

The National Council for One Parent Families welcomed the plans. Kate Green, the director, said: 'These are positive measures, and an important step forward for the many lone parents who want to work.'

Alistair Darling, the Secretary of State for Social Security, told an Organisation of Economic Co-operation and Development conference in London that tackling poverty among children was a priority for the Government.

'We know that children who grow up in poor households are less likely to do well at school,' he said. 'All too often we see this pattern of poverty passed down to the next generation; born poor, living poor and dying poor. That's what happens when governments ignore poverty.

'What is needed is the determination – and the means – to break that cycle of persistent poverty,' Mr Darling said.

You might like to contact the following organisations for further information. Due to the increasing cost of postage, many organisations cannot respond to enquiries unless they receive a stamped, addressed envelope.

Barnardo's
Tanners Lane
Barkingside
Ilford
Essex, IG6 1QG
Tel: 020 8550 8822
Fax: 020 8551 6870
E-mail:
media.team@barnardos.org.uk
Web site: www.barnardos.org.uk
Barnardo's works with over 47,000 children, young people and their families in more than 300 projects across the country. This includes work with children affected by today's most urgent issues: homelessness, poverty, disability, bereavement and abuse.

Brook
Unit 421, Highgate Studios
53-79 Highgate Road
London, NW5 1TL
Tel: 020 7284 6040
Fax: 020 7284 6050
E-mail:
information@brookcentres.org.uk
Web site: www.brook.org.uk
Brook is a professional non-profit-making organisation for young people up to the age of 25. It exists to enable all young people to make informed choices about their personal and sexual relationships so that they can enjoy their sexuality without harm. Helpline 0800 0185 023.

ChildLine
2nd Floor Royal Mail Building
50 Studd Street
London, N1 0QW
Tel: 020 7239 1000
Fax: 020 7239 1001
E-mail: reception@childline.org.uk
Web site: www.childline.org.uk

ChildLine is a free, national helpline for children and young people in trouble or danger. Provides confidential phone counselling service for any child with any problem 24 hours a day. Produces publications. Children or young people can phone or write free of charge about problems of any kind to: ChildLine, Freepost 1111, London N1 0BR, Tel: Freephone 0800 1111. Another Freephone number for children living away from home is Freephone 0800 884444 open Mon-Fri 3.30 pm-9.30pm and Sat-Sun 2.00 pm-8.00 pm.

Economic and Social Research Council (ESRC)
Polaris House
North Star Avenue
Swindon
Wiltshire, SN2 1UJ
Tel: 01793 413000
Fax: 01793 413130
E-mail: exrel@esrc.ac.uk
Web site: www.esrc.ac.uk
The ESRC is the UK's largest independent funding agency for research and postgraduate training into social and economic issues.

Family Education Trust (Family and Youth Concern)
The Mezzanine
Elizabeth House
39 York Road
London, SE1 7NQ
Tel: 020 7401 5480
Fax: 020 7401 5481
E-mail: trust@famyouth.org.uk
Web site: www.famyouth.org.uk
A national organisation with no political or religious affiliations. They produce leaflets, pamphlets, books, reports and video tapes on matters affecting the family.

National Council for One Parent Families
255 Kentish Town Road
London, NW5 2LX
Tel: 020 7428 5400
Fax: 020 7482 4851
E-mail:
info@oneparentfamilies.org.uk
Web site:
www.oneparentfamilies.org.uk
The National Council for One Parent Families has pioneered the development of 'return-to-work' training for lone parents. They produce publications including the recent *Returning to work: a guide for lone parents* and provide training courses. Ask for their publications list. Runs the Lone Parent Helpline: 0800 018 5026. Information for people bringing up children on their own (lines are open 9.15am-5.15pm on weekdays).

Policy Studies Institute (PSI)
100 Park Village East
London, NW1 2SR
Tel: 020 7468 0468
Fax: 020 7388 0914
E-mail: postmaster@psi.org.uk
Web site: www.psi.org.uk
Policy Studies Institute is one of Britain's leading research institutes, conducting research which will promote economic well-being and improve quality of life. PSI enjoys a reputation for the rigorous and impartial evaluation of policy initiatives, and the publication and dissemination of research findings is central to PSI's ethos.

INDEX

abortion
    in Northern Ireland 1
    and sex education 9
    and teenage pregnancies 1, 3, 4, 5, 7, 15, 16
age
    of first sexual experience 4, 11, 20
        and sex education 5, 12
    of lone parents 26
    of motherhood 3, 7, 8

babies, born to teenage mothers, health risks 2, 17
benefits, State, and lone parents 19, 24, 25, 30, 32, 34-5, 36, 40
birth rates
    decline in 8
    numbers of births outside marriage 7, 8, 17
    teenage pregnancies 1, 2, 3, 4
boys
    and sex education 10-11
    and under-age sex 20
    see also fathers

childcare
    and lone parents 35, 36
        government policy on 19, 20, 38, 39, 40
childless women, numbers of 7, 8
children in care, and teenage pregnancies 13, 16
cohabiting couples 8, 17, 31, 32
contraception
    and condoms 15
    emergency (after sex) 5, 8, 9, 15
    and first-time sex 23
    and government policies on young people 12
    and lone parents 30
    and sex education 5, 9
    and teenage pregnancies 1, 2, 3, 4, 7, 21
    and under-age sex 20
    young people's attitudes to 6, 7, 9, 13-14

disabled people, and sex education 10
divorce, and lone parents 26, 29, 31
doctors see GPs (general practitioners)
domestic violence, and lone parents 26, 30

education, and pregnant teenage girls 12, 18
employment
    and lone parents 25, 29-30, 35-6, 36-7
        reasons for not seeking work 39
ethnic minorities
    lone parents 27, 29
    in the population 8

families
    and teenage pregnancies 13, 14
    and teenage sexual activity 4, 7
family planning clinics 2, 7
fathers
    lone 26, 27, 31

and teenage parenthood 1, 2, 10-11, 12, 18
    ChildLine survey on 13, 15, 16
    and family attitudes 14
    statistics 1
girls
    attitudes to sex 22-3
    and electronic dolls 12, 21, 22, 23
    having under-age sex 7-8, 9, 20
    reasons for first-time sex 6
government policy
    on lone parents 19-20, 31, 32, 35, 37, 38
        and childcare 19, 20, 38, 39, 40
    on teenage pregnancies 1, 2, 3, 5, 6, 7, 12, 17, 19-20
GPs (general practitioners), and teenage pregnancies 2, 7, 14, 15

health risks
    and teenage mothers 4, 12, 17
    young people and unprotected sex 12
homelessness, and teenage pregnancies 14, 16

lone parents 24-40
    age of 26
    education and training for 37, 38
    ethnic minority 27, 29
    family size and age of children 27
    fathers 26, 27, 31
    government policy on 19-20, 31, 32, 35, 37, 38
        and childcare 19, 20, 38, 39, 40
    and housing 30, 35, 36, 37
    marital status of 26
    never-married 7, 8, 26, 27, 28, 29, 31
    outcomes for children 27-8
    and paid work 25, 35-6, 36-7
        employment prospects 29-30
        reasons for not seeking work 39
        and working families tax credit 35, 38, 40
    and poverty 24, 34-7, 40
    and relationship breakdown 30
    rise in births outside marriage 17
    separated 30, 31
    sexual attitudes and behaviour 30
    and state benefits 19, 24, 25, 30, 32, 34-5, 36, 40
    statistics on 26, 29, 31-2

marriage
    and lone parents 29-30, 31
    number of marriages 8, 17
    young people's attitudes to 6

parents
    of lone mothers 30
    and teenage pregnancies 14, 15, 18
Pill, contraceptive
    morning-after 5, 8, 9, 15
    and teenage pregnancies 3
poverty, and lone parents 24, 34-7, 40

Roman Catholicism, and young people in Liverpool 21, 22

schools, and sex education 5, 6, 12, 14
sex education 4, 10-11, 17, 22
    age of beginning 12
    and age of first sexual experience 5, 12
    in schools 5, 6, 12, 14
    and teenage pregnancies 3, 9
    and under-age sex 20
    and young people's attitudes to sex 6, 23
sexual abuse
    and teenage pregnancies 15-16
    and young people 10, 14
sexual relationships, young people's attitudes to 6-7, 14-15, 20, 22
sexually transmitted diseases (STDs), and teenagers 4, 7, 8, 9, 10, 20

teenage pregnancy 1-23
    and abortion 1, 3, 4, 5, 7, 10, 15, 16
    and children in care 13, 16
    confidentiality issues 15
    and contraception 1, 2, 3, 4, 7, 21
    getting help and support 14
    and girls' education 12, 18
    girls leaving care 10, 16
    government policy on 1, 2, 3, 5, 6, 7, 12, 17, 19-20
    health risks for teenage mothers 4, 12, 17

    and homelessness 14, 16
    reactions to being pregnant 15
    and sexual abuse 15-16
    statistics 1, 3, 4, 7, 10, 17
        international comparisons 2, 4, 11, 23
        local variations 1-2, 5
    telling parents 14, 15
    under 16s 1, 6-7, 10, 11, 21
        and abortion 3, 10, 15, 16
        and contraception 2, 21
unemployment, and teenage pregnancies 5

women
    age of motherhood 3, 7, 8
    unmarried 7, 8

young people
    attitudes to sex 6-7
        reasons for having sex 14-15
        and under-age sex 20, 22
    and sexual activity 7-8, 9
    and sexual knowledge 7, 9, 10
    and sexually transmitted diseases (STDs) 4, 7, 8, 9, 10, 20
    teenage pregnancies 1-23
young women see girls

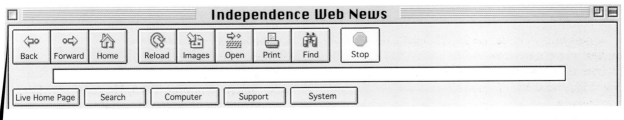

*****

The Internet has been likened to shopping in a supermarket without aisles. The press of a button on a Web browser can bring up thousands of sites but working your way through them to find what you want can involve long and frustrating on-line searches.

And unfortunately many sites contain inaccurate, misleading or heavily biased information. Our researchers have therefore undertaken an extensive analysis to bring you a selection of quality Web site addresses.

National Council for One Parent Families
www.oneparentfamilies.org.uk
On this web site you can find information including News Help desk and Factfile. Clicking on Factfile takes you to a list of links including Who are lone parents?, Children, Poverty, Sources of income, Housing and Policy Briefings. A very thorough web site.

Brook
www.brook.org.uk
Brook's web site was established in 2000 to help publicise the work of Brook. Brook provides free, confidential sex advice and contraception to all young people. You can choose from Frequently Asked Questions, Brook Guides and Under Sixteens. There is information on emergency contraception within the Guides link.

International Planned Parenthood Federation (IPPF)
www.ippf.org
www.ippf.org/mezzo/index.htm
The online guide to love and relationships. For young people, by young people. Supported by the IPPF.

One Parent Families Scotland
www.gn.apc.org/opfs
OPFS Scotland's National Voluntary Organisation Supporting Lone Parents. Within the Factsheets link there is a lot of information for lone parents from their Lone Parents Rights Guide including: Health, Money, Housing Issues and Going Back to Work.

New York Online Access to Health (NOAH)
www.noah-health.org
This site offers a US perspective on teenage pregnancy. Scroll to the bottom of the home page and click on Health Topics. Then click on the Pregnancy link. Then click on Teenage Pregnancy for a wide range of relevant articles.

Department of Health
www.doh.gov.uk/public/stats1.htm
Scroll to the bottom of the page and click on the Search link. Entering the words 'teenage pregnancy' will bring up a comprehensive list of government articles on the issue.

ACKNOWLEDGEMENTS

The publisher is grateful for permission to reproduce the following material.

While every care has been taken to trace and acknowledge copyright, the publisher tenders its apology for any accidental infringement or where copyright has proved untraceable. The publisher would be pleased to come to a suitable arrangement in any such case with the rightful owner.

Chapter One: Teenage Parents

Teenage pregnancy, © Crown copyright is reproduced with the permission of the Controller of Her Majesty's Stationery Office, *Live birth rate to women aged 15-19*, © Eurostat & Centre for Sexual Health Research, Southampton, *Rate of teenage pregnancies is highest for nearly a decade*, © Independent Newspapers Ltd, 2000, *Teenage sexual health*, © Brook, *Teenage conceptions*, © Brook, *Sex under sixteen?*, © Family Education Trust, *One in four girls doesn't wait till 16 to have sex*, © The Daily Mail, 2000, *The changing face of the family*, © Office for National Statistics (ONS), Crown copyright is reproduced with the permission of the Controller of Her Majesty's Stationery Office, *Lost innocence*, © The Daily Mail, 2000, *Teenage parenthood*, © Barnardo's, *Babies are for keeps*, © Jerome Monahan, *Dolls show realities of teenage pregnancy*, © Telegraph Group Limited, London 2000, *'I can't believe it's happened to me . . .'*, © ChildLine, *Calls to ChildLine*, © ChildLine, *Four births in 10 outside marriage*, © The Daily Mail, 2000, *Don't stigmatise teenage mothers*, © Policy Studies Institute (PSI), *Government launches £2m advertising campaign*, © Telegraph Group Limited, London 2000, *The bitter regrets of teenagers who had under-age sex*, © The Daily Mail, 2000, *The girls who do say no*, © The Daily Mail, 2000.

Chapter Two: Lone Parent Families

Single minded, © Diane Taylor , *One-parent families today*, © National Council for One Parent Families, *Lone parents by sex and marital status, 1995-1997*, © National Council for One Parent Families, *The growth of lone parenthood*, © Economic Social Reserach Council (ESRC), *Rise of the single mother*, © The Daily Mail, 2000, *Size of lone-mother families*, © Office for National Statistics (ONS), Crown copyright is reproduced with the permission of the Controller of Her Majesty's Stationery Office, *Mamas and the papas*, © Barbara Ellen, *Today's challenge – to end lone parent poverty*, © National Council for One Parent Families, *Family poverty*, © Office for National Statistics (ONS), Crown copyright is reproduced with the permission of the Controller of Her Majesty's Stationery Office, *Brown reforms lone parent aid*, © Guardian Newspapers Limited, 2000, *Childcare alone not enough to get lone parents back to work*, © Policy Studies Institute (PSI), *New nurseries to help single parents go to work*, © Independent Newspapers Ltd, 2000.

Photographs and illustrations:

Pages 1, 10, 15, 23, 26, 38: Pumpkin House, pages 6, 11, 16, 21, 24, 29, 33, 40: Simon Kneebone.

Craig Donnellan
Cambridge
January, 2001